How *Awesome* *this Place*

Genesis,
the ongoing Story of CREATION
as written
in the FIRST BOOK OF MOSES

PETER K. THOSS

Order this book online at www.trafford.com
or email orders@trafford.com

Most Trafford titles are also available at major online book retailers.

Note for Librarians: A cataloguing record for this book is available from Library
and Archives Canada at www.collectionscanada.ca/amicus/index-e.html

Printed in Victoria, BC, Canada.

ISBN: 978-1-4251-8457-5

*We at Trafford believe that it is the responsibility of us all, as both individuals
and corporations, to make choices that are environmentally and socially sound.
You, in turn, are supporting this responsible conduct each time you purchase a
Trafford book, or make use of our publishing services. To find out how you are
helping, please visit www.trafford.com/responsiblepublishing.html*

*Our mission is to efficiently provide the world's finest, most comprehensive book publishing
service, enabling every author to experience success. To find out how to publish your book, your
way, and have it available worldwide, visit us online at www.trafford.com*

 www.trafford.com

North America & international
toll-free: 1 888 232 4444 (USA & Canada)
phone: 250 383 6864 ♦ fax: 812 355 4082

*This Book is dedicated to my faithful Wife Eleanor
and her grown up children Lindsay and Sonoama,
their Spouses and her Grandchildren, Kelly, Hannah, Isaac and Aaron,
my also grown up Children, Jerry, Debbie, Rick, Steve and Jennifer,
their Spouses and my Grandchildren,
Nicole, Danica, Matthew, Amanda, Shelby and Miguel
as well as my Great Grandchildren Christopher and Alexander.*

OVER FOUR Billion Years have passed since the Beginning of the Story of Creation, here condensed into Seven Days in God's Time or subsequently into the "Day" God made Heaven and Earth (Gen.02;04).

While Scripture speaks of History in this enlightening Story, it does so without intend to calculate the Ages of this Planet in literal Years or Days in Mans Time.

The Story of Creation is a very universal Story. As much as all Religions of the World have some sort of perception in regards to the Origin of Things, the Reader may have his or her own believes in this direction.

The Writer acknowledges each persons right of Interpretation and does not wish to be controversial with his Point of view, but rather helpful in a meaningful manner.

This Book is written as a modern day Story. The Story of Creation can not be fully understood without certain acknowledgments.

Firstly, Faith comes first and then Understanding, not the other way around.

Second, Man must acknowledge the transient Power of God.

The Story of Creation speaks of this Power.

It speaks of transformation from spiritual Origin to physical Form and from multiplication on this Earth to indestructible spiritual Condition.

How awesome this Thought.

How awesome this Place. (Gen. 28./17)

As much as Scripture reveals itself to Man more and more with repeated Reading, as much is this Book designed in the same manner.

May the Reader be richly blessed by reading this Book.

THUS
THE HEAVENS AND THE EARTH
WERE FINISHED
AND
ALL THE HOST OF THEM.
Gen.02;01

HOW AWESOME THIS PLACE
Gen.28;17

IT IS HE WHO SITS ABOVE
THE CIRCLE OF THE EARTH
Isa.40;22

I HAVE SPOKEN AND
I WILL BRING IT TO PASS;
I HAVE PURPOSED AND
I WILL DO IT!
Isa.46;11

HEAVEN IS MY THRONE AND
THE EARTH IS MY FOOT-STOOL
Isa.66;01

THE FIRST BOOK OF MOSES
COMMONLY CALLED GENESIS

Ch. 01; 01 :
In the beginning GOD created the Heavens and the Earth.

IN THE BEGINNING
WAS THE WORD
AND THE WORD WAS WITH GOD
AND THE WORD WAS GOD.

HE, CHRIST, WAS IN THE BEGINNING
WITH GOD;
ALL THINGS WERE MADE THROUGH HIM
AND WITHOUT HIM
WAS NOT ANYTHING MADE
THAT WAS MADE.

These Words are very powerful Words:

GOD is the Creator through His Son, Jesus Christ.
The WORD is creative.

GOD has no Beginning – HIS Creation has.

This means, that GOD is NOT finished yet, that the Story of Creation is still an ongoing Process, that the Story of Creation is Alive and that the Story of Creation is a Story of TODAY.

Gen.
Ch. 01; 02 – 05:
02: The Earth was without Form and Void, and Darkness was upon the
    Face of the Deep; and the Spirit of GOD was moving over the Face of the
    Waters.
03: And GOD said, "Let there be Light "; and there was Light.
04: And GOD saw that the Light was good; and GOD separated the Light
    from the Darkness.
05: GOD called the Light Day and the Darkness HE called Night.
    And there was Evening and there was Morning, one Day.

The First Day:

GOD is a GOD of Order.
Disorder and Darkness speak of the presence of another Power (Tohu-wabohu).

The Waters speak of a life-giving substance, first Spiritually and then Physically.

Scripture teaches, that by the Spirit of GOD, the Arm of GOD moves.

Scripture also says, GOD is Light and there is no Darkness in Him. When the Apostle Paul saw Christ, he spoke of Light, brighter than the Sun.

We do not read, that GOD created Darkness.
We read, that Darkness was upon the Face of the Deep.

We read, that GOD created Light and that HE separated one from the other.

Only of the Light we read, that it was good.
In the book to the Hebrews we read:
"By Faith we understand that the World was created by the Word of GOD, so

that what is seen was made out of things which do not appear. (Heb.11;03)

We therefore see two conditions in the process of Creation, namely, that what is seen has its counterpart in the Spirit-world and that Darkness was already present before GOD brought Order by the Spirit of GOD into a state of Chaos (formless and waste).

Life comes from GOD, the originator of Death is the Devil.

Both Conditions existed at the Beginning.
Life and Death existed before Man did.

God offered Man Life, but Man fell for the other.
In other words, GOD can only provide – the Choice lies with Man.

Here, we see, that GOD brought Light into this World, but, that a Day consists of Light and of Darkness.
This means, that we live in a World with much Good and much Evil in it, but only by following the Light of this World, Jesus Christ, can Man triumph.

Gen.
Ch 01; 06 – 08:
06: And GOD said, "Let there be a Firmament in the midst of the Waters from the Waters ".
07: And GOD made the Firmament and separated the Waters which were under the Firmament from the Waters which were above the Firmament. And it was so.
08: And GOD called the Firmament Heaven. And there was Evening and there was Morning, a second Day.

The Second Day:

The Bible speaks of Heaven as more than one Heaven.

There is Heaven, the dwelling-place of GOD.
There are heavenly Places, of which Eden, also called Paradise is one of them.

There is Heaven above the Earth, here called Firmament.

The second Day deals with the Firmament, but it also deals with the Waters.

The Waters are described in two distinct Forms.
The Waters above the Firmament are spiritual Waters of Life and those below the Firmament are physical life-giving Waters.

The Apostle Paul says, that, which is firm is enduring and that which is infirm is not.
H2O is the infirm and the spiritual is the firm.

This Scripture teaches, that Man must separate the two, because GOD does.
It says, that GOD has made it so and that God identifies everything by its Name.

When Man was placed on the face of this Earth, he was placed here with certain pre-existing conditions.
This has not changed to this Day and Man would be wise to acknowledge what GOD has provided and conduct his Life accordingly.
GOD prepares ahead of Time.
GOD fully knows, what will be required.

Long before Life appeared by HIS Word, GOD prepared a great Heritage for Man.
GOD in HIS infinite Wisdom also prepared very complex life-supporting conditions on this Earth.

GOD calls Earth a dwelling-place for Man, but the other Planets a dwelling-place for Demons.
Man has trouble to understand this concept and is beginning to mix things up.

GOD calls everything by its name, but also shares HIS creativity with Man.
Pro-creation means co-creation.
This means, that as much GOD bestows upon Man procreation, as much

Man can not create Life on his own.

GOD calls the Firmament Heaven and this Earth, the Garden.
Jesus speaks of Eden as Paradise and the Apostel Paul speaks of Heavenly Places.
Man is well advised to pay close attention to what GOD has called everything.
Much meaning is attached to it.
This is reflected in the fact, that the word "good" is absent in the second Day.
Not, that things are not destined to be "good", but rather, that good things, such as Water can actually become a Flood.
We read of a Flood coming out of the mouth of the Serpent.

Here, we read, that God has prepared a dwelling-place for Man to be on save ground.
When Man follows good advice by God with mans GOD-given divine nature, Man is on save ground.
When Man follows the Serpent by his beastly nature, he is heading for Catastrophy.

Gen.
Ch.01; 09 – 13 :
09: And GOD said, "Let the Waters under the Heavens be gathered together
into one place and let the dry Land appear."
And it was so.
10: GOD called the dry Land Earth, and the Waters, that were gathered
together HE called Seas.
And GOD saw, that it was good.
11: And GOD said, "Let the Earth bring forth Vegetation, Plants yielding
Seed, and Fruit-trees bearing Fruit in which is their Seed, each according
to its kind, upon the Earth." And it was so.
12: The Earth brought forth Vegetation, Plants yielding Seed according to
their own kinds, and Trees bearing Fruit in which is their Seed, each
according to its kind. And GOD saw that it was good.
And there was Evening and there was Morning, a third Day.

The third Day:

The third Day deals with terrestrial conditions only.

"Under the Heavens ", means terrestrial.
We read in Scripture of terrestrial bodies and we read about celestial bodies.
Do not mix up the two.

Earth is terrestrial and Mars is celestial.
Man is ordained to live on this Earth and not on Mars.
Mars has a different purpose.
GOD created everything with a purpose.
Man is well advised to acknowledge this Fact.
Everything outside of this Planet Earth is adressed as Celestial.

When Man explores celestial bodies, he gains valuable knowledge about the material aspect of the Universe of God, but when Man ignores his destiny in the body of flesh and blood, he steps into otherwise uncharted waters and according to the story of Creation, is heading for nothing but troubled territory, not to speak of incredible waste of precious Life and Money.
As much as GOD is Spirit and reigns out of spiritual dimensions, as much is HE concerned with Life on Earth and conditions on Earth, simply because HE created them. HE created the Earth and the Sea long before HE created Man.
Throughout the Bible, we are made aware of the Importance of the Interactions between Land, Sea and the Atmosphere, here called "Firmament".

It may be questionable, that Man will ever fully understand the Complexities of this interdependent, sophisticated mechanism.
The modern Computer-age has yet to provide a functional formula in this respect.

Man has been busy with creating his own Biosphere, but has so far failed to sustain balanced conditions over a reasonable length of time.

Man discovers, that Nature is endowed by GOD with a multitude of biological clocks, working together in harmony to constantly restore balance in this complex system.

It is not, that GOD does not want Man to understand, quiet to the contrary.
Understanding promotes responsible behavior, not abusive one.
Understanding comes by acknowledgment of GOD and HIS Creation.
Only when Man gives Credit where Credit is due, namely to a supreme Creator, GOD, can Man walk in the right direction.
Man without GOD is messing things up. This is an observable fact.
GOD restores.
Man, who follows Christ, also restores.
When Man neglects to pay attention to his ultimate Creator, he encounters failure after failure, this also is an observable fact.
Only when Man conducts his Life in the Spirit of GOD, can he make spiritually wise choices.

This brings us to a much debated Controversy about this World and what is in it.
It is the theory of Evolution vs. the Story of Creation.
This is mostly due to Man accepting or not accepting Truth according to Scripture, which actually corresponds with scientific Observation when carried to Conclusion.

Here, we read, that GOD created every Tree, Plant and other Vegetation according to their Fruit and according to their Seed.
This means, that Creation by GOD is an ongoing process, because it has a Goal.
Evolution denies this Truth.
Evolution consents to an ongoing process, but denies the existence of any Goal.
Evolution subscribes to the Survival of the Fittest in the form of genetic Selection.
Only during the Time of relative recent History has Man gained most of his Knowledge about the Genetic Code and the building blocks of Life.

It is the writers considered Opinion, that due to this newly acquired Knowledge,
Man will be able to imitate Creation by an apparent process of creating Life.
DO NOT BE SHOCKED, because it will be imitation, NOT CREATION.

Creation has certain sustainable Goals.
It has the Goal to fit Life to the Circumstances and it has the Goal to make Man and Beast and Plant "good" at its Conclusion.
When the Lion lies beside the Lamb, he does not eat it.

The Bible tells us much about it.
It says, that all of Creation longs for the revealing of the Sons of GOD.

GOD sees ahead.
Before it is accomplished, GOD sees, that it is all good.
For a matter of fact, GOD saw that it was all good, long before it is done.

GOD's Creation does NOT terminate with the Survival of the Fittest, You can count on it.

GOD in HIS infinite Wisdom has destined for HIS Creation to be GOOD when HE started out with it and in spite of what we see now, to be GOOD when HE is done with it.
Granted, Faith in GOD and Jesus Christ is essential to grasp this Concept.

According to Scripture, Creation is an ongoing process, simply because GOD has a Plan which speaks of doing a New Thing (Isa.43;18-19).

GOD says;
I have spoken and I will bring it to pass;
I have purposed and I will do it (Isa.46;11)

We can observe Creation in Nature all around us.

It is evident, that many Species of Animals and Plants have perished and new ones are discovered every day.

Man is in need of Understanding, but Man must also realize, that he can not explain everything.
When it comes to the Issue of Life, Man will never fully comprehend it.
GOD alone holds the Patent to Life and imitation is not Creation.

However, GOD has bestowed upon Man certain Powers.
One of these Powers is Mans duty to assist, maintain and protect the Creation by GOD, also referred to as Environment.
Many books have been written in regards to this Issue.

Man has the capacity to explore and even alter the genetic Structure of biological Life, but he will also have to realize, that in the End, everything exists according to its own kind and will either perish or return to it, no matter what.

All things in this World, even if they are "forever" are limited to their own time.
In this case, we read of the "third day" as a day in GOD's Time.

Man, who is forever rebellious, will eventually pass away, testifying, that "forever" can actually be limited to the Life-span or Generations of Man.

The Bible speaks of "forever" in two ways:
"Forever", which speaks of the Indefinite and
"Forever", which speaks of the Infinite.

The Indefinite, although it is not known, has a Beginning and an End.
The Infinite on the other hand has NO End.

Only the Infinite is truly enduring, while the Indefinite is a Time-restricted Concept.

Understanding comes by separating these two distinct meanings.

The third Day speaks of GOD preparing a Garden for biological Life to come into Existence.

Gen.

Ch.01; 14 – 19:

14: And GOD said:

> *"Let there be Lights in the Firmament of the Heavens to separate the Day from the Night; and let them be for Signs and for Seasons and for Days and Years,*

15: and let them be Lights in the Firmament of the Heavens to give Light upon the Earth". And it was so.

16: And GOD made the two great Lights, the greater Light to rule the Day, and the lesser Light to rule the Night; HE made the Stars also.

17: And GOD set them in the Firmament of the Heavens to give Light upon the Earth,

18: to rule over the Day and over the Night, and to separate the Light from the Darkness. And GOD saw that it was good.

19: And there was Evening and there was Morning, a fourth Day.

The fourth Day

The fourth Day deals with Celestial objects and not too much with the Terrestrial ones.

As we said before, GOD is a GOD of order and HE provides according to the order of needs and according of how HE purposed things.

It does not say, that GOD created Light for this Earth on the fourth Day. What it says, is that GOD saw, that this Earth was in need of Light and that GOD made two great Lights to shine upon the Earth.

The existence of the Earth and the heavenly objects is not the Issue here; the Rule of the Order of the Universe is.

GOD speaks to Man with physical Pictures, but, the Bible teaches, that these physical Pictures have their counter-part in the Spirit-world.

Therefore, the Rule of the Order of the Universe speaks in many Ways.

It speaks in terms of things, that can be shaken as Terrestrial and it speaks of things, that can NOT be shaken as Spiritual.

The Apostle Paul speaks of Man being a Spectacle to the ruling Powers of the Universe (1.Cor.04;09 / Eph.03;10 / Eph.06;12 / Col.02;15/20).

This has two meanings or applications:
Physical Man is confined to Terra Firma, his dwelling-place, but what he does has an Influence on the ruling Powers of the Universe.
This makes Man a formidable Creature.

Here, we read of conditions on Earth before Man arrived.
We read, that GOD lightened up this Earth and we read, how GOD purposed it.

First of all, GOD has purposed, that everything physical, that HE has created, has its Time.
It is the spiritual or transformed condition which is "enduring".

The Physical, all of it, has a Beginning and an End, make no Mistake about it.

Second, GOD has purposed a separation of Things in their Time.
GOD is very precise in what HE does.
With GOD, there are no Mixups.
Mixups are a Tool of the Devil.
When Man follows the Rule of GOD, his (or her) Life reflect Order, not Mixups.

When we read of the Sun ruling the Day, certain thoughts come to Mind.
Jesus taught HIS Followers to walk in the Light of the Day and avoid the works of Darkness.
Jesus said: "I am the Light, remain in me, so that Darkness can not overcome you".
Jesus knows, that we live in an Age of spiritual Darkness.
A New Age is dawning where Mankind will see the Light and Things will be good.
During this Time now, a lesser Light will guide us, a Light of Faith, not of Sight.

GOD will reward those, who believe in HIS Light, namely Jesus Christ.
GOD will also reward those, who obey HIS Rule.

The Stars in the Heavens are part of this Rule.
Jesus was born under a special, shining Star.
Every Person on Earth is born under a certain, special Star.
The Reader may ponder this Issue further.

This does not mean, that Man should divide the Heavens and gaze at the Stars in order to predict his future (Isa.47;13).
This means, that all Things in the Universe transpire according to the Rule by which GOD has pre-ordained Everything.

Gen.

Ch.01; 20-23:

20: And GOD said, "Let the Waters bring forth swarms of living Creatures, and let birds fly across the Earth, across the Firmament of the Heavens."

21: So GOD created the great Sea monsters and every living Creature that moves, with which the Waters swarm according to their kinds and every winged Bird according to its kind. And GOD saw that it was good.

22: And GOD blessed them, saying,
"be fruitful and multiply and fill the Waters in the Seas, and let the Birds multiply on the Earth."

23: And there was Evening and there was Morning, a fifth Day.

The fifth Day:

Again, the fifth Day has two applications.
It has a Spiritual application and it has a Physical meaning.

When it comes to literal reality, the Bible and Science agree.
Life started in the Sea and progressed into the Air and in between.

Satan is called the Prince of the Power of the Air.
He comes as an Outcast out of Heaven, meaning, out of the Spirit-world.

What does this mean?

The Air and the Sea's are interconnected.
One can not support Life without the other.

When we read about the great Sea-monsters, we are made aware, that the Sea is not without hostility, neither is Land and Air.

We observe a long food-chain, where everybody eats everybody with the great Sea monsters at the top of it.

Why do we then read, that GOD saw, that it was Good?

We obviously read about prophetic Scripture.
We read of the Past from the view-point of GOD.
We read of an Age yet to come as an accomplished Fact.
We read of Creation as an ongoing process.
We read prophetic Scripture, which will most certainly be fulfilled.
The question is,"when?"
When Satan, the present Prince of the Power of the Air, also called, the Ruler of this World is locked up and Jesus Christ, the Light of this World commences HIS Reign.

This is Truth according to Scripture.

GOD proceeds with HIS Plan irregardless of Evil.

Evil is a Mystery.
Man can not fully understand it nor comprehend it.

Man can not eliminate it.
Man can only take sides.

Life comes from GOD's dimensions only.
Life will prevail over Death because it is blessed.

Although GOD's Creation is not finished yet,
GOD has blessed what HE has created and what is yet to come.
This is a valid reason to follow GOD's side in Christ, Jesus.
GOD's Creation is so powerful, that it takes unbelievable ignorance to ignore it.

When we read, that living Creatures "swarm" over the Earth, under the

Waters and in the Air, we read about the Principles of Life.

The Principles of Life are such, that Life exists abundantly or not at all.
There is no such Thing, as a little bit of Life.
When Man follows the Rule by GOD, he is very generous, not petty.
Scripture is very repetitive with this issue, so that Man may gain understanding.
Man will not find Life (biological Life) on Mars or any other Planet.
If there would have been biological Life on Mars, it would have existed abundantly.
It also would have left certain Traces behind, such as Gases and Oils.
But Mars does not pass the "Sniff-test".
Scientific Instruments can not sniff any Gases originating from biological Matter on Mars.
Only one piece of Evidence, how things are on Mars and how they are not.

We have to bear in Mind however, that physical Creation on Earth has Spiritual Goals.
Like it or not, This Earth is a testing ground for a great Reward.
When GOD is done with it, things are Good, meaning a final Age of this Planet with peaceful conditions, after which Millennium-time, Satan will have a last, however mysterious, kick at it. Perhaps to seal his final Demise.

Today, we still live in a World with both, Good and Evil in it.

To have Faith in GOD, means, to believe in a great Inheritance in another Dimension where things are Enduring and no longer perish.

This Earth has a Purpose, although a time-restricted one. (Only the New Earth will be enduring, because of Spiritual conditions.)
Creation teaches Man, that GOD is a very methodical GOD and that each Day is a stepping stone in the process of Fulfillment of GOD's Purpose.
Without each Day, without Day and Night, this can not be accomplished.

This is the fifth Day.
Only after the sixth Day will GOD rest.

Gen.

Ch.01 ; 24 – 31:

24: *And God said,*

  "Let the Earth bring forth living Creatures according to their kinds:
  Cattle and creeping things and Beasts of the Earth according to their
  kinds."

  And it was so.

25: *And GOD made the Beasts of the Earth according to their kinds and*
  the Cattle according to their kinds, and everything that creeps upon the
  Ground according to its kind.

  And GOD saw that it was good.

26: *Then GOD said:*

  "Let us make Man in our Image, after our Likeness; and let them have
  Dominion over the Fish of the Sea and over the Birds of the Air, and over
  the Cattle, and over all the Earth, and over every creeping Thing that
  creeps upon the Earth."

27: *So GOD created Man in HIS own Image, in the Image of GOD HE*
  created him;

  Male and Female HE created Them.

28: *And GOD blessed Them, and GOD said to Them,*

  "Be fruitful and multiply and fill the Earth and subdue it; and have
  Dominion over the Fish of the Sea and over the Birds of the Air and over
  everything living thing that moves upon the Earth."

29: *And GOD said,*

  "Behold, I have given you every Plant yielding Seed which is upon the face
  of the Earth, and every Tree with Seed in its Fruit;
  You shall have them for Food.

30: *And to every Beast of the Earth, and every Bird of the Air, and to every*
  thing that creeps on the Earth, everything that has the Breath of Life,
  I have given every green Plant for Food."

  And it was so.

31: *And GOD saw everything that HE had made,*
  And behold, it was very Good.
  And there was Evening and there was Morning, a sixth Day.

The sixth Day:

The sixth Day contains more Information than any other Day.
Perhaps, because this is the grand Finale in the Creation by GOD.

GOD spoke and it was so!

"It was so" testifies to a Beginning and an End.
It does NOT testify to anything that has BEEN.
What has BEEN is not the End of it all.

This is the great Mystery.

GOD says, it is the Beginning of a New Thing (Isa.43;19).
GOD has chosen to do things in Stages.

First, HE created all the Elements, here called "the Ground".
Then HE created Living Creatures out of the Ground by way of
Transformation.

The Elements are very uniform throughout the entire Universe.
Living Creatures on the other hand are very Individual, each of its own
kind.

We must differentiate between the two.
Man has discovered "Cloning". GOD abhors cloning.
GOD is a GOD who creates Individuality, respects Individuality and
expects Man to honor it.
Cloning lacks the ability to adapt to the Circumstances, meaning lack of
resistance to various viral attacks.
When the Bible speaks of attacks of wild Beasts, it speaks of these
conditions.

Man would be wise to pay attention to the Story of Creation.
It is meant to guide and protect Mankind.
To ignore the Word of GOD is not only foolish, it has dire Consequences.

This Chapter is a "Down to Earth" Picture.

It speaks of the Ground, the Earth and it speaks of the Living Creatures which GOD created out of it.

Now, behind this Picture of physical Creation, there is another Picture, a Picture with a Veil in front of it.

This is the Mystery of the Bible.

When Man has Faith in GOD, GOD allows Man to lift this Veil.
HE, GOD shows Man the Spiritual dimension of HIS Word.
By HIS Word, all things were created, be they Spiritual or be they Physical.
GOD is Spirit.

The Bible speaks of many different Living Creatures around the Throne of GOD.
GOD created them all and to HIS Glory they exist.

To live a Life outside of the Glory of GOD is equal to ignoring ones own Needs.

After we have read, how GOD created Heaven and Earth, we read about the Top of the Creation by GOD, namely Mankind.
We read of "us" and we read of "our likeness"
GOD said: *"Let us make Man in our Image".*

Why is that so?

The Bible speaks of GOD as Sovereign Deity, the only One, but it also speaks of GOD and His Word and HIS Spirit.

We read, that the Word was with GOD from the Beginning and that HIS Spirit brooded over the Waters.
We also read, that in the Beginning was the Word and that this Word is Christ, (Colossians 01; 15 – 17).

We repeat:
GOD is Spirit and those who worship HIM must do so in Truth and Spirit.
GOD is Light, a Light brighter than the Sun.
GOD is Love, a spiritual Love which is enduring (never-ending).
GOD is Just and there is no Injustice in HIM.

Much more can be said about GOD, but GOD can not be fully understood by Man.
Mans Understanding of GOD is limited to the Word of GOD.

Because of the Limitations which GOD bestowed upon HIS Creation and because of the Concept of a Beginning and an End (meaning all biological Life on Earth), we read of an "Image" and of a "Likeness" of GOD.

This means, that all physical Life is mortal and only the Spirit will endure. It also means, that the Physical is the Image of the Spiritual and that Man is the highest Order in this Concept.

When Man was created by GOD, GOD bestowed upon Man certain "Dominion" over all of Creation.
Dominion has the meaning of Stuart-ship, but also the meaning of Self-control.
It further says, that GOD gave to Man and Beast every green Plant on Earth for Food.
It says nothing about a licence to kill and eat each other, clearly speaking of prophetic Scripture.

The Writer is not a Vegetarian, because he realizes, that these Conditions are Conditions yet to come and that in this present Age, Animals eat each other and the Lamb wont last long in the presence of a Lion.
GOD's Covenant with Noah includes everything, that lives, as Food for Man, speaking of this present Age (Gen.09;03 / Acts 10;12 – 13).

However, even in this fallen Age, Man is not absolved of responsible Stuart-ship over GOD's Creation.
The Powers bestowed upon Man, make Man accountable to GOD.

Man did not create himself – GOD did.
Man did not create Beast and Plant – GOD did.

All biological Life on Earth progresses according to GOD's Plan, according to genetic programming by GOD,

but only Man is granted free Choices.
This means, Animals rely on Instinct while Man has both, Instinct and Intellect as well as a higher Spirit.

As strange as it may seem,
Animals are guided by their Instinct, but when Man follows his Instinct without his higher Spirit and his Intellect, he goes from one Disorder to another.
Mans Life depends on more than Instinct, it lies on a higher plain than that of the Animals (2.Peter 02;12 / Jude 10).

This is what this Story of the sixth Day of Creation is talking about.

When we talk about the "Image of God", we talk about GOD granting Man free Choices in his Life-style.
This does not mean, that Man is ordained to play God.
This means that God extends HIS never-ending Love to offer Man free Choices in his daily behavior.
Man has a very wide Latitude in his Lifestyles on Earth, but Man needs a connection to the Rule by GOD in order to be truly happy and succeed.

Free Choices, also means, that Man is the most powerful Creature on Earth, but nevertheless has certain Limitations.

On the other hand, GOD does not want back what HE has given.
That means, that GOD requires of Man to do the right thing and that HE is not going to do it for him (or her).
Mans GOD – given "Dominion" makes Man accountable to GOD.
Man has no longer any excuses, not to know.
Man can not get away with pleading Ignorance, Man will bear the Consequences for his actions.

Now, we come to an Issue in this Story with which Man has a lot of trouble.
It says: "Male and Female HE created them."
Man has NO Choices in this Matter although he wants to.

Without going into lengthy discussion on this Issue, we can not abrogate
Responsibility back to the Creator.

If we deny, that GOD created Man as Male and Female, we place ourselves
in opposition to GOD and the Order of HIS Creation.
This is a very serious Issue, because the Generations of Man depend on this
Concept.
It does not say, that Man is forced to multiply, not at all.
What it says is, that in Order to multiply it takes two to tango, two different
Sexes, that is.
The word "Dominion" speaks of controlled conditions.
Uncontrolled Conditions do not come from GOD and may not qualify for
GOD's Blessings.
The Evidence is all around us.
The so-called Love of the depraved Mind is mostly short-lived, ending in
Disaster.
The orderly Love between Male and Female has GOD's Blessing.

When the Human being departs from the Order by GOD, GOD hands
them over to strong Delusions.
More and more Humans have trouble with their sexual Orientation as
prophesied in Scripture.

In the Beginning, Man and Woman knew who they were and they knew
each other.
Over the Millennia's, Mankind has gone astray and many have surrendered
to their own Passion's.

The Order of Male and Female is a very basic Order by GOD and there
are absolutely no Provisions in either GOD's Word or GOD's Plan for
tampering with this Order.

GOD made it so.

GOD ordained it so.

GOD does NOT ordain a Contradiction in the Human being, the Devil does.
The Devil is a great Imitator.
He cleverly imitates Love by pretending.
He holds passionate Love out to Man (and Woman) like a carrot before a donkey.
The beastly nature within Man eats the tasty carrot, but is never satisfied by it.
He or She is only graving for more and more carrot's.

There is NO such thing as sexual Union between same sex Partners.
There is only a Pretend.

The human Right is only right when it is in harmony with what GOD has made Right.
When so-called spiritual Leaders ignore the Creation by GOD, they have elevated the human being above the Order of GOD.

The Bible has prophesied this Condition.
It speaks of conditions like in the days of Noah.
When the Bible speaks of conditions like in the Days of Noah, it speaks of the end of this Age.
In the same breath, it also speaks of a wicket Generation and it calls Man to flee it.
(Acts 02;40)

Man obviously has the capacity to step out of the Image of GOD and do his or her own thing.
Man on his own is destined to fail, make no mistake about it.
Only in the Image of GOD can Man truly succeed.
Only in the Image of GOD can Man be on save ground.

While Man has many Choices, in this he can only take sides, one side or the other.

When GOD created Man as male and female, HE has bestowed upon them

a very complex system of needs and emotions.
This means, that in order to accept each other without fully understanding what GOD has ordained, both sexes need a connection to the Lord.

Without this connection to the Lord, both of them will have trouble with this much needed acceptance and will be faced with many unexplained disappointments.

Man and Woman on their own can not avoid these disappointments.
GOD does not disappoint.
GOD has provided. HE has provided a blessing to Mankind, but Man must accept, what GOD has provided. GOD will not force it on anyone.

To be "fruitful", foremost means to be fruitful in the fruits of the Spirit.
The two most important fruits are Love and Service.
Man is quick to concede to Love, but Service is another matter.
On the word "Service" the Spirits part. But Christ came into this World to be a Servant, and so must we.

Why do matrimonial Relation-ships fail?
Because Love has waxed cold, because Service has died.

The Devil is the originator of Death. It suits him fine, when the Marriage has died.

Those, who serve themselves, only fool themselves, they serve the Devil.
Those, who serve each other, serve GOD.

We also see another important Concept in the Story of Creation.
Repeatedly, we read about this "Dominion" issue.
A certain "Dominion" by Man over all Life on Earth shall prevail.

This is a much misunderstood issue.
Dominion, means control; foremost Self-control by Man and Woman, according to Scripture.
Now, it stands to reason, that Man (Woman) has to have control over his (her) Live first, before he (she) can control anything else.

When Man and Woman go ahead and multiply in an uncontrolled manner, they violate an important concept in GOD's Creation, meaning, they create Disorder for themselves and their offspring.
This goes for all phases in Mans Life.

GOD ordained Man to run things on Earth according to HIS Plan.
GOD gave Man "Dominion", meaning HE does not want to take it back.

When Man excuses his Failures by claiming, that it was not meant to be, he abrogates his Obligations back to GOD, but GOD does not want it back.
GOD expects Man to do the right thing and HE will most certainly hold Man to account.
This means, that GOD will not stop Evil in its track, not yet.
Scripture indicates, that Evil has to reach a certain full measure before it will be judged.
This also means, that from the Beginning of all things, GOD has devised a Plan of Salvation from Evil.
This Plan will also be fulfilled.

This is very, very serious business.
By granting Man "Dominion", Man is given Free Choice, free Choice to decide which side to take.

The Bible says; let the Evil be Evil and the Righteous be Righteous.
Right from the Beginning, we find Blame-shifting in the human race, but GOD will not accept it.
Each Person is accountable for his or her own actions, although maturity may come into play.
Therefore, to be accountable for ones own actions and to expect others to be accountable for their's, is sound biblical advise for having peace of mind.

Then, we find another important physical, as well as spiritual Law in the Story of Creation.
That Law is the law of Multiplication, which is also a Divine Principle.

First of all, GOD does not send HIS Word out to come back empty.
GOD send's HIS Word out to come back with multiple Result's.

This Earth is a Garden where things multiply according to their Seed, be it Fruit or be it Weed.
In this Age, both are here and they are here to stay.

The Word of GOD is called the Tree of Life and also the Water of Life.
The Devil seeds Weed and his Water is identified as a Flood.

Man is destined to till the Garden.
What will multiply in this Garden depends on what Man will do.

This is the Story.

Throughout the Bible, we read, that GOD will reward Man double or many times for spreading HIS Word, but we also read, that GOD will repay Man double Measure for any of his Deeds.
It say's, that all Deeds by Man on this Earth (Garden) will follow him to the other side and they will determine whereabout's he is going.

Between this Side, the Garden and the other Side, Eden, stand's the Cherubim with a flaming Sword.
A Flaming Sword is another Symbol for GOD's Word.

Man must become a Sword-swallower (eat HIS Word) to have access to Eden, also called Paradise.
A Cherubim is a Spirit-being.
Man need's to re-acquire his Spirit-condition in order to acquire a great Inheritance. The Bible tell's us much about it.

Interestingly, in the final part of Day Six in the Story of Creation, we read about a World with peaceful Conditions.
Then, we read again about GOD giving Man Dominion over HIS Creation on this Earth.
We read of Food for Everything, that creeps upon the Earth and has the Breath of Life.
We do not read about any Hostilities. It speaks of Harmony.
It says, that GOD saw that it was "Good".

The important Question now arises:
"Is this a Picture of prophetic character or is this a Picture of a prior World as it once existed?"
Has there ever been a Time of serenity and peace during the entire existence of this Planet Earth, when and where everything was "Good?"

The Apostle Paul says, that all of Creation is in Waiting (Rom. 08;19-25).
Paul speaks of things yet to come.
Jesus Christ says, He is the guarantor of a better World to come.
Scripture says ; GOD has purposed it and so it shall be (Isa.46;10-11).

"Shall be", means something yet to come.
What is yet to come has not been here yet.
Paul also says, that Jesus Christ is the second, but higher Adam (1.Cor.15;45)
Adam, means Man or Son of Man.
Jesus Christ became Man to fulfill this Picture.
When Jesus Christ died on the Cross, He said: "It is fulfilled".
Until then, it was not fulfilled. It was held in Abeyance.

The second Story of Creation, which we will examine later, says, that GOD created Male and Female (but not at once, neither does the first Story).
It only says: "Male and Female, HE created them", also meaning, Christ first, His Bride second.

What does this mean?
It means, that hostilities have existed long before Man came into the Picture.
It means, that the "Serpent, the Devil" was present long before Man was.
It does not say, that Man was the originator of Death.(1.John 03;08).
It says,that the Devil is the originator of Death.

When we read in Romans, Chapter 5, that Sin came into the world by one Man and Death through Sin, we also read, that the Devil is the father of Lies and that Man, who ignores GOD and Jesus Christ is easy prey for the Devil.

All pardonable Sin is committed in the Flesh.

31

If Sin is committed in the Spirit, it belongs to the Netherworld of Darkness, not to this World (2. Peter 02;04).

The good News is this :"For as in Adam all die, so also in Christ shall all be made alive" (1.Cor.15;22).
By speaking of "All", it obviously includes Adam.

So, we see, that all Mankind is mortal in the flesh and that all Mankind depends on GOD and HIS Son, Jesus Christ to provide Life in a Spiritual Condition.
Before the "Fall", Adam had free access to ongoing Life in Eden (Spiritual Condition).
After the "Fall", Adam (Man) is subject to GOD's Pardon in Christ Jesus, the only Provision for GOD being everything to everyone, everyone who accepts the "Water of Life" (1Cor.15;28).

Gen.
Ch.02;01-03:
01: Thus the Heavens and the Earth were finished and all the Host of them.
02: And on the seventh Day GOD finished HIS Work which HE had done, and HE rested on the seventh Day from all HIS Work which HE had done.
03: So GOD blessed the seventh Day and hallowed it, because on it GOD rested from all HIS Work which HE had done in Creation.

The seventh Day.

The seventh Day contains the most powerful Testimony that it is a Day yet to come.
It confirms everything in the foregoing six Days.

In the fourth Chapter of the Book of Hebrews, it states, that there remains a Sabbath-rest for the Children of GOD (Heb.04;09).
Of the present Time, the Bible speaks of a lifelong Bondage (Heb.02;15).

The proclaiming of the Gospel of Jesus Christ precedes the seventh Day and testifies to the Fact, that GOD is presently very busy with building HIS

House (John 05;17 / Heb. 03;06 / 1. Peter 02;05).

When the last one of a predetermined Number of Souls has entered His House, the Works is completed, finished and the Day of Rest shall begin, from which Time on, there is no longer any lifelong Bondage.

The Bible speaks on many occasions in the past tense, when it clearly also speaks of a Time yet to come.
This is, because the Bible is a Book of Prophecy among other things, has more than one Dimension and speaks of what GOD says as a done thing.
It also shows the same Picture irregardless of the Age in which Man exists.

In the Book of Revelation, we read:
"Now, I saw when the Lamb opened one of the seven Seals..."
It speaks of the past and the present in regards to the same Event (Rev.06;01).
Then it says:
"When the Lamb opened the seventh Seal, there was silence in Heaven for about half an Hour" (Rev.08;01).
This gives Evidence, that a Day which is yet to come, appears as a done thing, because of the Concept of Prophecy.
Only when there are no further Seals, it speaks of the Past.

Here, in the Picture of the seventh Day, there also are no further Days and we read of it as in the past, although it is a prophetic Picture.

This Concept is of certain Importance in order to better understand Scripture.

There is no point arguing about the literal applications of Scripture, because Scripture makes no claims in this direction (Rom.02;29).
Scripture claims to be the inspired, true Word of GOD and is mostly concerned with conveying Divine Truth to Man.
When reading Scripture, one must be very careful in paying attention to what is actually written without adding or subtracting anything to it.

Scripture uses Pictures and Illustrations in conveying divine Truth to Man.

It is more concerned with Man's spiritual well being than with material blessings.

Jesus Christ speaks of sacred Secrets being revealed to the Believer, while certain Illustrations are concealed to the Unbeliever.
Understanding comes to the person who has Faith in GOD, not the other way around.

This respectfully means, that literal Words can not be applied in the literal sense where spiritual Truth's are adressed.
For instance, Jesus said:
"Destroy this Temple and I will rebuild it in three Days".
The Apostle John said, we live in the last Hour.
In Revelation, we read of the second half of this last Hour, where there was silence in Heaven, before (first half Hour) there was War.

So, we see, that when we read the Story of Creation, we must study the entire Scripture in order to gain maximum Understanding.
Perhaps, that is why we find two Stories of Creation in the Book of Genesis.
One Story to illustrate the Ages and the other Story to illustrate what went on in these Ages, meaning with Man, GOD and the ruling Powers in the Universe.

It is the Writers humble desire to assist the learned Reader in adding to his (her) happy Journey through the Story of Creation and further amend his or her own Opinion in regards to this important Story.

The first Story of Creation ends with GOD resting on the seventh Day, but it also speaks of the Heavens, the Earth and all the Host of them, meaning the Ruling Powers in the Universe.
This indicates, that we are still IN the Story of creation, including what the Apostle John calls the last Hour. This is NOW.

What is interesting to note however is the fact, that it does NOT say; and on the sixth Day GOD finished HIS Work.

It says: "And on the seventh Day GOD finished HIS Work which HE had done..."

It may be save to conclude, that GOD indulged in certain finishing touches on the seventh Day.
It does NOT speak of a strict no Work Order.
It speaks of a divine Principle of Work and Rest.

Jesus said: "The Sabbath is made for Man, not Man for the Sabbath".
Jesus acknowledges Man to be the highest Order in GOD's Creation.
Man however, needs GOD's Blessing.

GOD has promised to grant HIS Blessings to those, who abide by HIS Order of Things and obey HIS Commandments.

Furthermore, the transition between each Day does not happen with a Bang.
There is a twighlight zone between them, perhaps for Man to prepare.

GOD grants Man a wide Latitude in his Behavior on this Earth and it stands to reason that HE expects Man and Woman to do likewise with his fellow Man.

Comparable Translations:
* And on the seventh Day GOD ended HIS Work which HE had made...
  from Latin
* And on the seventh Day GOD finished HIS Work which HE had done...
  Holman Study Bible
* By the seventh Day GOD had finished the Work which HE had been doing...
  New International Version
* And by the seventh Day GOD came to the Completion of HIS Work that HE had made... *New World Translation*
* Und also vollendete GOTT am siebten Tage seine Werke die ER machte...
  German Luther Bibel
* Da brachte GOTT am siebten Tage Sein Werk, dass ER geschaffen hatte zur Vollendung... *Dr. Herman Menge, German*

The second Story of Creation

U NLIKE THE first Story of Creation, which is mostly a down to Earth Story, the second Story speaks of the Heaven's and the Earth, meaning, a spiritual Sphere and terrestrial Conditions.

The Heaven's are the Spiritual.
The Earth represents the Material.

It teaches Man, that everything that exists and everything that happens has its Origin in the Spirit-world.

Gen.
Ch. 02; 04 – 07:
04: These are the Generations of the Heaven's and the Earth when they were created.
In the Day that the Lord GOD made the Earth and the Heavens,
05: when no Plant of the Field was yet in the Earth and no Herb of the Field had yet sprung up – for the Lord had not caused it to rain upon the Earth, and there was no Man to till the Ground;
06: but a Mist went up from the Earth and watered the whole Face of the Ground –
07: then the Lord GOD formed Man of Dust from the Ground, and breathed into his Nostrils the Breath of Life; and Man became a living Being.

The first Verse in this new Story of Creation speaks about the Generation's of the Heaven's and the Generations of the Earth.

Notice the Plural.
When it comes to the Generation's in GOD's Creation, we read of the Plural the same as we read of the plural only when we speak of Saint's. (We find no such thing as a Saint Paul or Saint Peter in Scripture)

When we are advised to save ourselves from this wicked Generation, it applies to all Generations of mortal Man.

GOD has HIS own Numbers.
The Bible is not written to reveal all of GOD's Numbers, it is written to reveal GOD's Plan (Eph.01;10).
When Man attempt's to calculate GOD's Numbers, he only makes a Fool out of himself.
Starting with Adam on this Earth, we already read of Generation's, meaning Mankind.
When GOD spoke to Abraham, HE spoke in terms of "Thousand Generation's" (1.Chron. 16;15).
The Psalmist also speaks of "Thousand Generation's (Ps. 105;08).

This means, that no matter how intense Man searches for his own Generation's he will only find Remnants.
This is, because there are Numbers beyond the observable, GOD's Numbers.
GOD's Numbers in HIS Creation are sacred and secret.
GOD's Numbers will never be known in their fulness.

To calculate the Ages of this Planet and Mans Generations by way of Scripture is an Unbiblical Undertaking.
Even Science has its Limitations, because it would have to look into GOD's Mind which would mean, to look into Infinity.

GOD has given Man an atomic Clock to study HIS Creation, but not without its Limitations.
There are Dimensions beyond the Atomic Clock and Genetic Code, which, according to Scripture, Man will never unlock.
GOD has given Man the Faculty of Faith to deal with Godly Issues.

Faith is not contingent on Man's Intelligence.
All have GOD's invitation to Treat.
Without Faith, Man can not fully understand.
Without Faith, Man can not please GOD.

Science has great Value, but it deals with the Observable only.
This Scripture here speaks of Conditions which go beyond the Observable,
only Faith will do.
Because, Man has different decrees of Knowledge and Understanding,
particularly over the Ages, the Word of GOD has been written in simple
Terms and Illustrations, so that all of Mankind can benefit from its
Contents.

The works of Salvation is very complicated, just as Life itself is very
complicated, but it is also very simple, so that everyone can grasp and accept it.

So, it is with the Story of Creation.
It is very complicated and it is conveyed in simple terms and language.

Here, in this Scripture, we read of the Heavens and the Earth when they
were created.
What does this mean?
This means that the Goal is set in the Heavens and the Results are
manifested on this planet Earth.
Evolution has no Goal – Creation has.
Evolution speaks of survival of the Fittest.
Creation speaks of a Plan by GOD where Plant, Beast and Man adapt to
the Circumstances with the Goal, that in the conclusion all things will be
Good.
This may not be obvious at this Time, but this will be accomplished, You
can count on it.

The first Story and the second Story of Creation have one Picture in
common, namely that of the Heavens and the Earth.
It is the same Picture, because it speaks of what was Not, what Was, what Is
and what will Be.

What was Not, was Order on the face of the Earth.

What was, was the Word and the Word was with GOD and the Word was Christ.

What Is, is Creation in progress with biological and spiritual Goals (incl. Gospel).

What will Be, is the fulfillment of GOD's Plan, where GOD say's:
"Behold it was very Good".

As long as things are not "very good", Creation is still in progress (Isa.43;19).

Study the Gospel of Jesus Christ and find out more about it.

The opening Chapter of the Gospel by the Apostle John elaborates extensively on this Issue. Believe it!

Here, we read of "the Day" that the Lord God made the Heavens and the Earth, when beforehand, in the first Story of Creation, we read of "six Days" of Creation.

This is, because beforehand, we read of "History".
Here, we read of "Conditions in History", first Spiritual and then Physical – in that Order.

The "Lord GOD" and the "Word of GOD" are synonymous.
The Bible says: "In the Beginning was the Word and the Word was with GOD".
This means, that before any Life appeared on this Earth, the Conditions for Life pre-existed.
This is a Mystery to the spiritually un-discerned.
They look for Life on Mars or on Asteroids in the Universe.

This, of course, in itself is an Absurdity, because, even if Life would be found on Mars or on other cosmic Matter it would not answer the Question; how did Life get there?
Who prepared the Earth to sustain Life on it ?
Who designed the Genetic Code – and so on.

Man may unlock the Secrets of the Genetic Code and other building blocks of Life, but Man will not unlock the Secrets of Eternal Life.
Only GOD holds this Patent.
Only through transformation by the "Word", Jesus Christ can Man achieve this Condition.
This goes for all Generations over all the Ages, here condensed into the "Day that the Lord made the Heavens and the Earth".

Then, this Scripture goes on to speak about the Complexity of conditions to sustain Life on Earth.
Volumes of Books have been written on this Subject, but the actual implications only come to light, when Man attempts to create his own Biosphere.
He runs into one Obstacle after another.
Man is a Duplicator.
He tries to duplicate, what GOD has created, but he lacks the Formula.
This Scripture should open Man's Understanding, because it speaks about GOD's Formula.

Before anything can grow and before things are ready for habitation by Man,
GOD has a Mist go up from the Earth.
This Mist from GOD waters the Ground.

This has far reaching Implications.
When Man ignores the Importance of this Mist, namely the Spirit of GOD, he is lacking the most important Ingredient in his Undertakings.

Man wants to take everything literal.
He believes, that a literal Mist will do the Trick.
To the Disappointment to those who take everything literal, it wont work.

When Man has no spiritual Agenda, Man is doing things on his own and he is going nowhere. He encounters Failure after Failure.

Without this spiritual Mist, the Ground remains a spiritual Dessert.
This Scripture reminds Man, that as much as the literal Ground needs

literal Water to sustain Life, as much does the spiritual side of Man need this Living Water to sustain spiritual Life.

Man however has a Choice.

He can grovel around the Dust of the Earth or he can conduct his Life in the live-giving Spirit of GOD.

This is the Meaning of this Scripture.

But, this Scripture also speaks of Hope.

There is Hope, because Man did not form himself, GOD did.

GOD gave him Form.

GOD shared HIS Breath with Man. Can Man understand It?

Man therefore has two Natures.

Man has a Spiritual Nature, that which is from GOD and

Man has a materialistic Nature, that which is from the Ground.

This means, that Man has higher Instincts and that Man has lower Instincts and that he has the capacity to choose, to which one he caters most.

The Bible is very repetitive with this Issue.

The Bible also concerns itself mostly with spiritual Issues, because only with the Spirit, the Breath of GOD can Man have Life eternal.

All other Life goes back to the Ground from where it is taken, meaning all biological Life goes to perdition.

In regards to the "Spiritual", we read of many definitions. We read of Jesus Christ,

The Word of GOD,

The flaming Sword,

The Sword out of HIS Mouth,

The Breath of HIS Mouth, The Bread of Life,

The Water of Life,

A great Voice,

The sound of the Voice of Thunder,

A silent Hush.

The Spirit of GOD has many Functions.

It speaks with great Authority, the Voice of Thunder and it appears in a silent Hush, meaning it is very sensitive with its presence.

Man became a living being, also means, that Man has many functions.
Man can be very creative in the Spirit of GOD or he can proceed in his own Spirit or he can be outright destructive.
Man has this Power, but only in the Spirit of GOD can Man truly succeed.

Gen.
Ch. 02;08-09:
08: And the Lord GOD planted a Garden in Eden, in the East; and there HE put the Man whom HE had formed.
09: And out of the Ground the Lord GOD made to grow every Tree that is pleasant to the sight and good for Food, the Tree of Life also in the Midst of the Garden, and the Tree of Knowledge of Good and Evil.

This Picture speaks of "Eden", the "Garden", GOD and Man and whatever else is in the Garden.
We read of physical Form and we read of spiritual Condition.
Man in the Garden belongs to physical Form.
GOD and Eden speak of spiritual Condition.
GOD is Spirit and Eden (Paradise) is spiritual.
The Garden is physical, but has spiritual origin.
Man is also physical, but also has spiritual origin – from GOD.

Because of Mans innocence at the Beginning, Man had unrestricted access to Eden, the spiritual.
It does not say, that Man was physically immortal.
That would be a contradiction, because it would mean that Man was in the Spirit, like GOD.
What it says, is that Man had free access to the Tree of Life, meaning Life eternal without condemnation.

We must realize, that eternal Life was assigned to Man in the Spirit, the Image of GOD, not in the body of Flesh and Blood (John 03; 5-6).
In his physical nature, Man was already time-restricted.
Everything physical is always time-restricted, even when it is portrayed as

"forever".

Only in the spiritual is it truly enduring.

This physical Earth will perish, make no mistake about it (Isa.65;17 / Isa.66;22 / 1.Cor. 07;31 / 2.Pet.03;10-13).

When Scripture speaks of a New Heaven and Earth, it also speaks of the Old as having passed away (Rev.21;01).

This physical World has something to do with the originator of Death, the Devil (Matt. 04; 08-09).

GOD is a Creator and can not be stopped by the Devil.

GOD has the Power to transform (2.Cor.04;07).

GOD has transformed the Powers of the Spirit into physical Form, but HE will also provide a transformation into the Spirit through Jesus Christ.

In the Midst of the Garden, meaning this Earth, we find the Tree of Life, but we also find the Tree of Knowledge of Good and Evil.

It stands to reason, that in order for Good and Evil to exist, both, Good and Evil were already present on this Earth, long before Man came into the Picture.

Man did not bring Evil into this World, the Prince of the Power of the Air did.

Man did not bring Good into this World either, the Prince of Peace did.

Knowledge speaks of choice, to get to know one and the other.

Knowledge, means to have to answer in regards to what one knows.

A Child can not answer in respect to what the Child does not know.

Therefore the Kingdom of GOD (Eden / Paradise / Heaven) is freely accessible to the Children and the feeble of Mind.

Jesus said; the Kingdom of GOD is theirs.

When we read of two specific Trees, we read of two specific Conditions.

No-one of sound Mind would think of literal Trees.

The Tree of Life comes first.

The Tree of Life provides spiritual Food, not physical Food.

These Fruits are Love and Service. Without Love and Service no-one will see GOD.

The Tree of Life has other Fruit's as well.
The Bible speaks of Joy, Patience, Kindness, Goodness, Faithfulness,
Gentleness, Self-control, Obedience to GOD, Righteousness and Truth.

We are encouraged to eat these Fruits, practice them.
When we depart this World, they will go with us to the other Side.
They will not burn up. They will not perish.

The Tree of Life has also many Leaves, such as
Thankfulness, Gratitude, Unselfishness, Endurance, Steadfastness,
Long-suffering, Forgiveness, Tolerance and whatever else has Blessings
from GOD.
The Bible speaks of Healing by these Leaves and Fruits.
Truth and Truthfulness by themselves provide much of this Healing.

Man may find Truth outright painful, but it takes exercise in Truth to set
Man free.

Unfortunately for Man however, he lives in a World with much Good and
also much Evil in it and Man has to deal with either one of them, whether
he likes it or not.
Jesus himself had to suffer in this hostile World and for the Believer to
expect otherwise would be folly.

Those, who proclaim the possibility of perfection in this World, lead Man
astray.
Only in a transformed condition by the Power of GOD can Man reach this
Goal (1.Cor. 13;09-10).

The Tree of Knowledge of Good and Evil has not died.
As long as Man is held captive in the Flesh, he has to contend with it.
No-one on Earth, who is capable of making Decisions, can avoid it.
According how Man decides to act, will be his Destiny.

As we said before, Mans Deeds will not disappear, be they Good or be they
Evil, they will have Results.

The Tree of Knowledge of Good and Evil contains Death, because evil Deeds can not withstand the Light of GOD and have a way to blot the good ones out.

This is why Man needs a Redeemer to redeem him from getting blotted out.
Jesus Christ is this Redeemer.
He will redeem a repentant Heart.
The Unrepentant will die in their Sins and will have to give account.

This is a very serious Issue, because Eternal Life does not exist outside of Eden.

The Garden is a Testing-ground and in the End,
Man will be found on one Side or the other.

Gen.
Ch.02; 10 – 14:
10: A River flowed out of Eden to water the Garden, and there it divided and became four Rivers.
11: The name of the first River is "Pishon"; it is the one which flows around the whole Land of "Havilah", where there is Gold;
12: and the Gold of that Land is good;
Bdellium and Onyx stone are there.
13: The name of the second River is "Gihon"; it is the one which flows around the whole Land of "Cush".
14: And the name of the third River is "Tigris", which flows east of "Assyria". And the fourth River is the "Euphrates".

Before Scripture continues with Man and his World, it digresses to a Picture of prophetic character in History.
It does so, in Order to shed light on the actions by Man and the powers to be.

Remember, Eden is synonymous with Paradise.
Eden is a Heavenly Place, not confined to any particular Time in History.
Jesus said: "Today, you will be with Me in Paradise" (Luke 23;43).
We shall come back to this issue.

The Garden is GOD's provision for Man on this Earth.

What this Scripture explains, is, that the Water, meaning the Water of Life, is available to Man, Man whom GOD placed into the Garden.
The connection between the Garden and Eden is the Word of GOD, incarnate in Jesus Christ.
Jesus told His followers, that from His body flow Rivers of Living Water and that the same River of Living Water flows from the Body of those, who believe in the Works of Salvation.
These are the things, of which we read here in this Scripture and throughout the entire Bible.

Salvation is easy to understand, but those, who believe, that the Kingdom of GOD is simplistic are mightily mistaken.

While immutable Truth's are conveyed to Man in simple Illustration's, the Kingdom of GOD is no less complex, than Nature all around us.

Understanding of Scripture comes to Man slowly and haste is a tool of the Devil.
GOD is a very patient GOD and Man does well to be patient also.

Without patient verification of Truth, Man falls short in his ways of Understanding.
In todays Computer-age, Man is sadly deprived of patient verification of Truth.
Instant gratification and instant answers are the expectations in todays Societies.
Man, to his detriment, is more concerned with the speed with which he can obtain Information, than with the validity of the source of it.
This allows the Devil to fill todays Information-highways with horrendous Impurities and false Source-information, the purpose of which is to lead Mankind into deranged Life-styles.

The Bible has prophesied these conditions and is therefore alerting perceptive Man to Satan's hideous agenda.
Satan also has a Water, his Water is described as a Flood, not as a River.

His Flood is designed to sweep Man away.

Todays Societies are swept away by an ever increasing Flood of synthetic Information.

Knowledge on a material level multiplies with in-comprehendible speed and Internet, the "Web of the Woman" makes it easy picking.

Scripture tells us, that GOD works in a different fashion.

HIS Word does not change.

HIS Water of Life flows as a very reliable River within its banks in an eternally controlled way.

We read about this River on more than one occasion.

GOD provides HIS Word, so you can hold your ground in a very deceptive World.

The Bible says, that when Man ignores GOD's Word, this River dries up and Mankind is in serious trouble.

The Bible offers help in every situation.

Trust the Word of GOD and refuse to get caught up in the Worldwide Web, the *"Web of the Woman"*.

All Knowledge will pass away, make no mistake about it (1. Cor. 13;08).

Jesus warned, that if you gain all Knowledge and gain all Riches, but neglect your Soul, you gain nothing.

The Apostle Paul speaks in identical terms.

Here, we read, that the River of Water flows out of Eden.

Remember, Eden is spiritual and a destination for all, who have Faith in GOD and Jesus Christ.

Also remember, the Story of Creation is a prophetic Story among other teachings.

Here, we read, that this River out of Eden divided and became Four Rivers.

What does this mean?

It means four great Time-periods in the History of Mankind while it also refers to terrestrial Locations.

The River does not divide in Eden.

It divides after it has come out of Eden.

In other Scripture, we read about the four corners of the World or the four beasts on this Earth, indicating certain aspects to History.
We conclude, that the River of Living Water comes out of a spiritual dimension and provides this Water in terrestrial Locations and Times.

The First Time-period referres to a time of Milk and Honey.
It speaks of Gold, it speaks of Gemstones and it speaks of pleasant times and things which were good. It does not speak of Immortality, but of a long and good Life.
Obviously, in the Beginning, Man lived in a Land of plenty, also called a Garden where GOD walked, allegorically speaking.
This condition is still engraved into Mans mind and he is forever looking for a Land of plenty.

Strange, as it may seem however, History teaches, that when things are favorable for Man and times are good, Man forgets about GOD and worships the Golden Calf instead of GOD.
This progresses to the point, where Man stores up evil deeds so as to arouse the anger of GOD.
It does not literally speak of the Wrath of GOD here, but it implies this condition because the Second Time-period appears to be the immediate Time-period after the Flood.
The location of Cush reveals this secret.
It was a Time-period of rapid re-population of the Earth, a time of what we now consider "Ancient Civilizations".
Archaeological evidence testifies to this Time-period.
To the credit of modern Man, much effort is devoted toward the study of such evidence.
Rapid population-growth is also a sign of our times and the reader may ponder the implications connected with these issues further.

The Third Time-period seems to be connected with Times of great Conquest and Wars.
The Assyrians were a warlike and conquering people.
Perhaps modern Man still belongs to this Time-period as it has not come to its conclusion yet.
Man is in the midst of War-conditions, no matter how much he speaks of Peace.

The Fourth Time-period is the Time-period at our doorstep, because it referres to the "Euphrates River".
This has many implications.
We read in Scripture about Waters of the Euphrates River drying up.
This reliable prophecy has literal meaning and is has spiritual meaning.
When the literal Waters of the Euphrates are beginning to dry up, the worst Trouble in the entire History of Mankind shall occur.
Jesus has said so and the book of Revelation speaks about it (Rev.16;12).

The literal drying up process will most likely be caused by ever increasing irrigation projects upriver combined with un-favorable climate-changes.
This by itself will be much of the cause of Trouble at the beginning of it.

The Euphrates, when it flows, flows also through the countries next to the Holy Land or what at prior times belonged to the Holy Land.
This corresponds with much Prophecy in Scripture, which tells us more about these upcoming events which will have worldwide implications.

The other serious implication of this Time-period of this fourth River, is the proverbial implication of the Waters of Life drying up.

When this happens, and the Signs are already in the making,
Mankind will enter its darkest hour.
History will be in utter Darkness.
The Church will loose its Shine and Power.
The Sun will loose its Shine, literal and spiritual.

Remember, it started in the East, where the Sun rises and it ends in the West, where the Sun loses its Shine.
Jesus, the greatest Prophet ever, has spoken about this Time and Man has no excuse, not to know, when it actually occurs.
Jesus Christ is the only Hope, Man has in this hostile World.

HE says; remain in the Light, that this Darkness will not overcome you.
p.s. to Vs.11 and 12:
> *Archaeological findings as of late seem to suggest, that remnants of structures dating back to the First Time-period, are those, now found*

around the Mediterranean as much as 36 meters(118 ft.) below present day Sea levels.

Sea-levels have obviously varied considerably over the Millennia's, particularly at the end of the last Ice-age.

Civilizations at prior Time-periods existed predominantly at lower elevations and who knows, if and where the ancient story of "Atlantis" could fit in.

(Information according to the Times of London, January 2002)

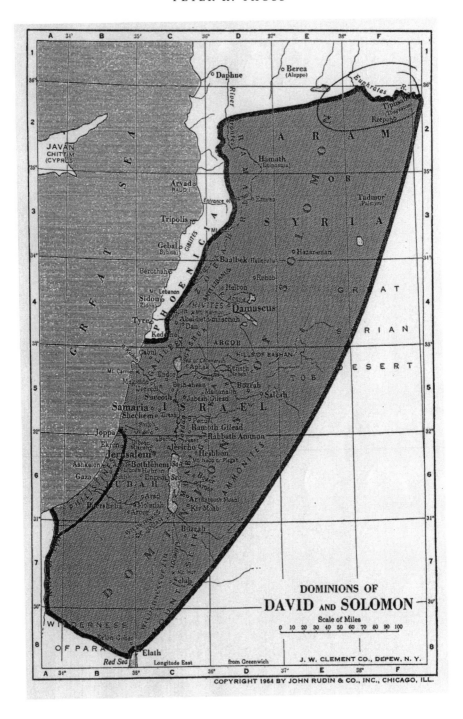

DOMINIONS OF
DAVID AND SOLOMON

Scale of Miles
0 10 20 30 40 50 60 70 80 90 100

J. W. CLEMENT CO., DEPEW, N. Y.

COPYRIGHT 1964 BY JOHN RUDIN & CO., INC., CHICAGO, ILL.

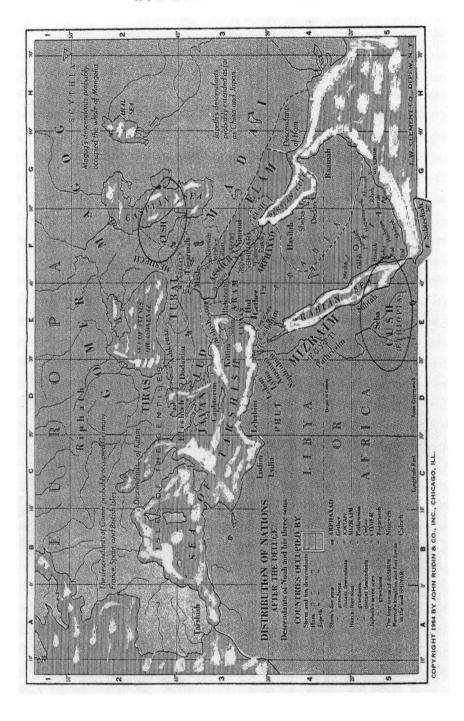

Gen.

Ch.02;15 – 17:

15: *The Lord GOD took the Man and put him in the Garden of Eden to till it and keep it.*

16: *And the Lord GOD commanded the Man, saying, "You may freely eat of every Tree of the Garden;*

17: *but of the Tree of Knowledge of Good and Evil you shall not eat. for in the Day that you eat of it you shall die.*

Now, Scripture continues with the Story.

We find this Principle on many occasions.

Scripture interrupts a Story to provide the reader with a Warning, a Wake-up call or other explanatory information.

This is GOD's way to communicate to Man important issues and Man is well advised to pay attention to it.

Also, when we find Repetition in Scripture, we find more than one meaning.

Here, we read, that GOD placed Man in charge of the "Garden", not Eden, not the Universe; the "Garden".

This further corresponds with GOD bestowing upon Man certain "Dominion".

Man seems to have a lot of trouble with this Concept.

Man is running "TO" and "FRO" to proclaim his rights to this GOD given "Dominion", but when things go wrong, Man is quick to abrogate this "Dominion" back to GOD.

"It was an accident", Man will say.

"It was not meant to be", we will hear.

However, "to till and keep it", means to take charge of things and not wimp out on GOD given Duties.

GOD will provide in need, but HE expects Man to "till the field", so he can eat.

GOD has instituted with Man a system of Work and Reward, not to make Mans life miserable, but to grant Man a sense of accomplishment and to give Man certain co-responsibilities.

The Apostle Paul minced no words, when he said:
"Those, who refuse to work, shall not eat". (2. Thess. 03;10)

Here, in this Story, we make an interesting observation.
GOD gave to Man certain Commandments before Man had done anything wrong.
This obviously means, that Man had a certain pre-disposition since Time immorial, to get himself into trouble.
Trouble does not come from GOD.
Trouble comes from the desires of the Heart.

When the desires of the Heart are in opposition to GOD's trouble-saving Commandments, Man gets himself into grave Danger.

While the Bible says, the Wages of Sin is Death (Rom. 06;23), it also says, there is Sin which is not mortal (1.John 05;17).
Therefore, Death is the result of disobedience to GOD by Man following the Prince of the Power of the Air, the evil one.
Only the Prince of Peace, Jesus Christ has the Power to deliver Man from Death.
Only Jesus Christ provides access to the Tree of Life.

Another Lesson is this:
GOD allows no punishment to happen without Warning, but
GOD's Warnings do not go on forever.
Scripture says, that after three or four serious Warnings, GOD hands Man over to strong Delusions.
In other words, there may be a time, when Man runs out of lifelines.
This Scripture here encourages Man to stay on save ground and not to play around with promises by the great Serpent.

GOD sets the Rules, not Man.
When Man follows his own Rules, he follows Rules, which are not spiritually discerned. He follows carnal Rules.
Carnal Rules do not provide spiritual, eternal Life, they terminate in Death eventually.
Only GOD's Rules, spiritual discerned Rules, lead Man in the right direction.

It does not say, that Man brought Death into the Garden.
Life and Death existed long before Man did.
What it says, is that Man is given a Choice.
Man has a Choice. He can trust GOD and follow His Rules and
Commandments or Man can ignore what GOD has provided and eat from
the Tree which is good to look at.
The Prince of the Power of the Air is not always ugly.
He deceives Man with many things which are good to look at.
He works and deceives on a physical level.
Knowledge is Power on this earthly Realm.
Knowledge is the opposite to Ignorance and Ignorance is not Bliss.

So, what is the Problem?

The Problem is, that with Knowledge come Obligations.
Man enters a state of transformation from Innocence to Accountability.
Man becomes obligated to do the right thing and GOD can no longer do it
for him.

When the Child has come to make his (or her) own decisions, the Parent
can no longer do it for him (or her).
He or she will reap the Consequences for what he or she does.

So it is with all Mankind.
To the decree of Knowledge of what is Good and Evil, Man is accountable
for his actions, in this instance here, accountable to a Holy GOD.

Scripture points out, that GOD is just and there is no injustice in Him.
Man is unable to bear the Consequences for his own injustice.
Jesus Christ did Justice for Mans Injustice.
Jesus Christ suffered Death in place for Man.
Without a Redeemer, Mans fate is sealed – in that Day.

This is the meaning of this prophetic Scripture.

Gen.
Ch.02;18:

18: Then the Lord GOD said, "It is not good that the Man should be alone; I will make a Helper fit for him".

This Verse is a stumbling-block to modern Man and Woman, but it does contain divine Truth, wether Man and Woman like it or not.
It is not so much a picture of the Sexes, as it is a picture of a divine Principle, namely, that of Service.

Christ died for You and me and he was a Man.

Scripture is always alive and applicable now.
Scripture is not written to entertain or to humor Man with old fashioned Fables.
Scripture, by its own evidence, is written to provide Man with guidance throughout his own Life and to provide Information in regard to GODs Plan.

The Kingdom of GOD is of a Spiritual nature and therefore all of Scripture has spiritual applications.
The Bible is also the wisest Book in the World.
It teaches much about the Law of Cause and Effect among other physical Laws and spiritual Laws.

For Instance: "Every action has a reaction" is a physical Law as well as a spiritual Law.
Man can pay attention to these Laws or Man can simply ignore them, but one thing Man can absolutely not do, he can not avoid them nor can he get around them.
Man will bear the Consequences, no matter what he will do.

The Bible also shows both sides, that of GOD and that of His opponent, the devil.

Here, we read, what GOD says.
GOD says, Man needs help.
The devil says, Man can do it by himself.

Man is ordained by GOD to help each other.
The devil tells Man and Woman, that they are not each others Servant.
But, here we read of the Mastermind-principle.
Man did not invent it, GOD did.
However, GOD started with the Family.
Man applies the Mastermind-principle in his business first and forgets about his Spouse.
How can the Spouse be a "Helper", when the Spouse is un-informed.
For the Spouse to be fit to help, it is essential to be informed.
How many Families break down, because the Spouses are un-fit to help each other.
Communication is sadly lacking.
Spouses must agree to inform each other of all and any on-goings in their Life in order to succeed with their Relationship.
This should most definitely happen, before the Relationship commences.
The parties must evaluate each other to the decree by which they are fit to help each other besides being "Good to look at".

This is the Issue of this Scripture.
Do not ignore it.
You can not have harmony in Your Life without it.
Your future Spouse will NOT improve. At least, do not count on it.
He or She is either "Fit" or "Unfit", make no mistake about it.

What is the Test?
The Test is "Stress" and "Money".

The Bible speaks much about Money, but what is Stress?
Stress is the condition of Adversity.
How a person behaves in conditions of Adversity and Distress reveals his or her true Character.
Help comes from a patient person, NOT from an angry one.
Haste is a tool of the devil.
Avoid impatient People, they go from one Trouble to another and have little help to offer.
The other Test is Money.
On the Issue of Money, the spirits part.

Fairness and Honesty with Money can not be compromised upon.
A stingy Spouse is a life-long aggravation, a dishonest one an outright
disaster.
Either side has to be willing to provide help in need.
One-sided Relationships will never be whole.

However, in all of this, GOD did not appoint us to be alone in our troubles.
Even, if a person lives alone, she or he should associate with others in a
helpful manner.
Christ taught the Principle of service for a reason, the reason being, that
only Servants are found to be in Heaven. The devil will have all the others.

Unfortunately, the World is full of selfish, un-serving people. Stay away
from them.
You can not win with a selfish, unconscionable person; You can only avoid
them.
Without being judgmental, the Apostle Paul writes, that "Faith is not
everyone's business". With some people, the devil has a heyday.

A Helper, means a loving Servant.
Love and Service are essential to fulfill GODs Will.
Love and Service are an antidote against depression and disappointment.
Severe depression and disappointment are the most common cause of
suicide.
Suicide shows an alarming increase in todays World.
Accepting help from a Servant of GOD (angel unaware), means accepting
GODs formula for enjoying Life.

Life is very precious to GOD, simply, because HE created it.

To be a joyful Servant in the Kingdom of GOD, means to be a loving
Servant from one person to the other.
Disharmony between people has its origin by ignoring what is written
in the Word of GOD, by ignoring what GOD has ordained from the
Beginning.

GOD is Love.

A loving Servant is patient and kind, not jealous or a bragger,
 not arrogant or rude, not self-seeking, not irritable, not resentful, not
rejoicing in the wrong, but delighting in the right.
He or she bears all things, believes in all things, hopes in all things,
endures all things (1. Corinthians, Chapter 13.)

All the foregoing we find in this Verse 18.
It is a reliable formula for a Life in Harmony between people and between
people and GOD.

On the positive side, the Bible says, that by accepting these Concepts,
relationships can be restored and made to work.

Will Man take heed and understand?

Gen.
Ch.02;19 – 20:
19: *So out of the Ground the Lord GOD formed every Beast of the Field and
    every Bird of the Air, and brought them to the Man to see what he would
    call them; and whatever the Man called every living Creature, that was its
    name.*
20: *The Man gave names to all Cattle, and to the Birds of the Air, and to
    every beast of the Field; but for the Man there was not found a Helper fit
    for him.*

Why do we read, that no Helper, fit to help, was found, right after we have
read of the Promise by GOD to provide such a Helper?

It is one of the Mysteries in the Kingdom of GOD.
GOD is not a GOD of immediate Gratification.
GOD is a patient GOD and He wants Man to be patient also.

Man can not have it both ways.
Would GOD not be patient with Man and delay certain promised actions,
Man would have no Time to mend his ways and Mans Faith in GOD would
be of little Value.

When GOD makes a Promise, there is a certain Test in store for Man.
GOD is testing Mans Faith.
No Faith exists without first being tested.
Man does not particularly like it that way, but that is the way it is.
The Scoffers are quick to point it out and ask; where are the actions by
GOD?
The Scoffers do not understand, that GOD rewards persistent Faith and not
the expectations by Man.

To reward someone for something, which is not accomplished yet, is a huge
Mistake.
GOD does not make such a Mistake.
GOD carries out, that which He has purposed, but He does so according to
His Plan and not according to Mans Plan.
Things do not always come to pass for Man, the way he would like to,
 but rather after he has fulfilled certain Duties.

The foregoing Verses speak of these Duties.
They do not speak of the order of Creation. The first Story did that.

Here, we read of Mans association with every Beast, Bird and living
Creature.
We read, that Man is not only ordained to name every Creature on Earth,
but we also read of Mans Duty to fearlessly identify, that which Man finds
within his carnal Nature.
Anyone who has doubts about his or her lower instincts, does not have to
look any further than his or her own Soul.
The ancient Civilizations in the far East were very much apprized of these
facts and confront Man with these very attributes to this Day.
Even Times are identified accordingly.
There is the Year of the Pig, the Snake and whatever Animal fits its Time.

The Writer has no intentions to validate the Zodiac and other Calendars,
but rather draw attention to biblical Truths and to assist Man with his
understanding of his sometimes inexplicable nature and behavior.
Needless to say, that the Lamb and the Lion are an incompatible
combination in this present Age and this Age is what this Scripture is

talking about.

The Millennium-age will have different conditions.

Scripture teaches, that in order for Man to control his carnal Nature, he must be willing to identify it; name it.

The book of Revelation says, Man must measure himself, the Temple (Rev.11;1-2).
GOD will not do it for him and neither is there any possibility to be free of it while here on this Earth.
Man and Beast are mentioned together on many occasions, because both of them are formed out of the Ground and both have the Breath of Life from GOD in them (Gen. 01;30), but only Man has a spiritual nature, called here, the Image of GOD.

This Scripture calls for the spiritual nature to have Dominion over the carnal nature, also called animalistic nature.
This is an individual Duty and nobody can do it for someone else.
Unfortunately, this means on the Issue of Self-control, not much help is available. Man must discipline himself.
Self-discipline is essential to accomplish anything.

It is very interesting to note, that all of this is written before the "Fall of Man".
This indicates, that these conditions existed on Earth at all Times and that the Garden and Eden (Paradise) are not the same Place nor the same Condition.

Gen.
Ch. 02; 21 – 22:
21: So the Lord GOD caused a deep sleep to fall upon the Man, and while he slept took one of his Ribs and closed its place with Flesh;
22: And the Rib which the Lord GOD had taken from the Man He made into a Woman and brought her to the Man.

This is a spiritual Picture and this is a physical Picture, because it speaks of a "deep Sleep" and it speaks of the "Flesh".

It also speaks of "Bone".

What is the Meaning of it all?

As we have said before, the Bible is alive and for it to be alive it has to have present Day applications.
This Picture speaks of Man and it speaks of Woman, meaning, it speaks of Mans sexuality.
A deep Sleep is a condition ordained by GOD.
It is a condition whereby Man does not exercise his Will or controls his actions.
It is a suspended state of Existence, a state of Innocence if You will.

The Bible speaks of Jesus Christ as the second Adam and of this Picture here, as the first Adam.
Jesus Christ, the second Adam had some growing up to do.
He did not appear in a physically completed State.
Adam, the first Adam also had some growing up to do.
He also did not appear in a physically completed State.
He was formed by GOD from the Ground, just as other Creatures were formed by GOD from the Ground and received the Breath of Life.

This means, that there is a Time during which Man (and also Beast) is sexually asleep.
GOD ordained this condition to grant Man a state of innocence and to prepare Man for the next stage in his Life.
During this state of innocence Man is unaware of the other Sex.
This is a very precious state of existence in Mans Life and those, who violate this state of innocence, will have to deal with GOD directly, because an innocent Child is an automatic Citizen of the Kingdom of GOD.
Jesus Christ said:
"Those who cause one of these little ones to sin; It would be better for him to have a Millstone fastened around his neck and to be drowned in the depth of the sea".
(Matthew 18;06.)
These are very powerful words and yes, they are spoken by Jesus.
Those, who preach an all forgiving Jesus, better not overlook this Scripture.

There is Sin for which Man has to account, because it is deliberate Sin against GOD and His Order.

A deep Sleep is not something to be tempered with by Man.

GOD has a Time for sleep and GOD has a Time for awakening.

Man has little control over his sexual awakening, GOD has.

When Man violates the ordained Order by GOD, Man may be guilty of arousing a certain Anger by GOD and that is one of the worst things, Man can do.

The innocent human being is entitled to a state of protection by those in charge.

The World is full of violence in these "Last Days", largely due to neglect by Mankind in regards to the innocent Children, not even to speak of the yet unborn.

The yet unborn are destined to praise the Lord (Ps.102;18) and those, who interfere with birth, interfere with the Generations of Man, which is a very serious Issue.

The Generations of Man depend on Procreation. (Although with Man in control).

This story here speaks of the Beginning of Procreation.

GOD created Man and Woman with the Purpose of Procreation, not Man and Man.

Only Woman and Man are fit for Procreation.

Only Woman and Man can join in this Task.

When Man awakes out of his Sleep, he finds Woman.

He finds a Mystery, but close to his Heart.

It does not say, that Man woke up and understood what happened.

It says, that Man accepted her as part of himself and adored her.

He did not try to understand her. Only by accepting what GOD has done as a Mystery, can Man and Woman fully enjoy each other.

Gen.
CH.02;23 – 25:
23: Then the Man said,

"This at last is Bone of my Bones and Flesh of my Flesh; she shall be called Woman, because she was taken out of Man".

24: Therefore, a Man leaves his Father and his Mother and cleaves to his Wife, and they become one Flesh.

25: And the Man and his Wife were both naked, and were not ashamed.

Now, we look at the Result of what happened.
We see a Story, which repeats itself throughout the entire Bible.
It is a Story of Unity before GOD.
As much as GOD is a GOD of Order,
He is also a GOD of Unity.

GOD teaches Man in this Story, that this much desired Unity does not come without a Price.
We read, that Man has to give something up, something from Himself.
Man has to make a certain Sacrifice.
This applies to everyday Life.
In order to be successful in Family-relations, the parties must be willing to strive for Unity and they must be willing make certain Sacrifices.

This Principle also has spiritual meaning in that it applies equally to the Membership in a Church.
Christ is not taken out of the Church, the Church is taken out of Christ.
Christ not only gave His Rib, He gave His Flesh and Blood and His Rib was broken.

This is a very powerful Story, a Story of Sacrifice, Unity and Re-unification.
Christ accepts His Bride (the Church) as part of Himself, because He loves her and she is taken out of Him.
If Man would like to benefit from this Story and have a successful Marriage, he must abide by the same Principle.
GOD has given here His un-equivable Underwriting for Success.

The Bible does not Speak of liberation of one Sex from the Other.
The Bible speaks of Unity between the Sexes, and those, who willfully destroy this Unity reap a bitter Harvest.

There is no selfish Behavior in this Story.
It is a very pleasant Story of acceptance of one by the other without criticism.
It does not say, that there was Perfection.
What it says, is that there was Acceptance.
Rejection is a Tool of the Devil.

When we read, that Man leaves his Parents to form a new Unit of Family with his Wife, we do not read, that Man should forsake them.
It all is about going from one Unit of Family to another.
It does not absolve Man and Woman from honoring Father and Mother.
That is a Life-time Command by GOD with the Promise of a lifetime Blessing.

In this enlightening Story, we also read, that Marriage was instituted by GOD long before any Religion took root on this Planet.
This means, that Marriage is a Global Institution and Man is well advised to heed this Order by GOD irregardless of his or her Believe-system.

The final Truth is portrayed as a "naked Truth".
This means, that in order for a Marriage to last, a Marriage has to be built on Trust.
It is a sure Recipe for Disaster, to marry someone, whom You can not trust.
Both Sexes must be naked, means both Parties must be Open and Exposed to each other, not only one of them.
Not to be ashamed, implies, that they must be comfortable with each other in this "exposed" condition.
They must be on save Grounds with each other. They should be able to discuss even the most delicate Issues with each other, without either one of them taking any Offence.
If these Pre-requisites are not present, prior to a Union, the Parties are most definitely unfit for Marriage with each other. The "Good Book" says so.
The other implied Lesson in this Story is this:
It is absolutely not possible to cover up before GOD.
Man and Woman can cover up with each other, but are always exposed before GOD, who can see through Flesh and Bone and Mind.
The Bible advises Man and Woman not to do anything shameful.

To ignore the Eyes of GOD is utter foolishness.

Finally, this Story speaks of a very powerful Love, as there is no greater Love than sacrificial Love between Man and Woman and between GOD and Man.
Does Man get the Message?

Gen.
Ch.03; 01:
Now, the Serpent was more subtle than any other wild Creature that the Lord GOD had made.

This Verse adresses the nature of the Serpent.
We shall list other descriptions of the Serpent:

"Abad-don", Angel of the bottomless Pit.	(Job 26;06 / 28;22 / Ps.88;11 /
"Apollyon" in Creek	Rev.09;11)
"Accuser" before God and "Satan"	(Job 01;06 / Rev. 12;09)
"Adversary" and "Devil", the prowler	(1.Peter 05;08)
"Be-elzebul" or Belzebub", blasphemer	(Matt. 10;25)
"Be-lial", worthless, lawless	(1. Cor. 06;15)
"Deceiver of the whole World"	(Rev.12;09)
"Destroyer"	(1. Cor. 10;10)
"Devil", associated with Demons	(Matt. 04;01 / Eph. 06;11-12)
"Dragon"	(Isa.27;01 / Rev.12;03 / 13;04)
"Enemy"	(Matt. 13;25 and 39)
"Evil one"	(Matt. 06;13)
"God of this World"	(2.Cor. 04;04)
"Imitator of an Angel of Light"	(2.Cor. 11;14)
"Liar and father of lies"	(John 08;44)
"Oppressor"	(Isa. 16;04)
"Prince of the Power of the Air"	(Eph. 02;02)
"Ruler of this World"	(John 12;31)
"Satan, ancient Serpent"	(Rev. 12;09)
"Tempter"	(Matt. 04;03)

Because we read, that Satan the great Serpent disguises himself as an angel

of Light, the Church-fathers gave him the name
"Lucifer", the shining one (Lucis or lucius – Light, Ferre – to bring).

All of this means, that the Devil has many Functions, here summed up as
"subtle, cunning and crafty".
The Devil approaches Man in a subtle way.
Jesus warned Believers to avoid those, who are cunning and crafty, because
they may be Servants of Satan (Eph.04;14).

Before we commence to examine these opposing spiritual forces in the
following Verses, we are made aware of the nature of the Serpent and his
devious attributes.
The Serpent was here long before Man was here and is therefore
unavoidable for anyone in this present Age.
Jesus had to contend with him and so do we.

Unfortunately, not many Sermons are heard on the subject of the Serpent
and his craftiness and the Devil likes it that way, but the Bible calls on
diverse occasions for fearless identification of the Devil and his different
functions, because, we read here, that the Devil likes to ambush Man and
that he does so in a very subtle way.

We have read before, that the carnal nature within Man is comparable with
all sorts of animals on this Earth.
Here, we are made aware, that the Serpent, which is at the bottom of
them all, is actually on the top of them all when it comes to craftiness and
deception.

This is powerful Metaphor, because when those from the bottom wind up
on the top, Man is in serious Trouble.
So, watch out, when the yeast is coming up (Gal.05;09).

Second part of Gen
Ch.03;01:
He said to the Woman, "Did GOD say, You shall not eat of the Tree of the
Garden?"

Here, we read how the Trouble begins.

It begins with a very serious Question in regards to the "Word of GOD".

Not only is it bad enough, when Man quarrels over how one should interpret the Word of GOD, but it is outright deadly when Man denies or doubts what GOD has to say.

Digressing from what GOD has to say, has always dire consequences.

Scripture speaks in many ways, but what GOD has to say, never changes.

It is not, whether Scripture is to be applied Literal or Spiritual, which undermines the Word of GOD, it is rather the questioning of divine Truth which accomplishes the Devils Goal.

Scripture, in most instances, has more than one meaning and more than one application, but divine Truth is always to be found in the Word of GOD.

Read Scripture and understand it according to how GOD reveals it to You at the Time.

GOD speaks to the six year old the same as He speaks to the sixty year old.

GOD is fair and speaks to Man according to his understanding and the capacity thereof.

The Apostle Paul compares it with drinking Milk or eating solid Food.

Both are of great Value in any ones Life.

Here, we see the great Deception.

Should you believe GOD?

Does GOD really exist?

Does GOD really care? Why should you not enjoy yourself and follow your own Desires?

read on!

Gen.
Ch.03;02-03:
02: And the Woman said to the Serpent,
*   "We may eat of the Fruit of the Trees of the Garden;*
03: but GOD said, 'You shall not eat of the Fruit of the Tree which is in the
*   midst of the Garden, neither shall You touch it, lest you die'".*

This is what is meant by the word "subtle".

The Devil is not without strategy. He first gets the Woman to agree with him on certain issues. Second, he attacks at the weakest spot.

By the weakest spot, it is not meant to be arguable, whether Woman is the weaker sex or not. It could just as well be a Man, who is the weakest spot. It is the "Weakest spot", which is the salient point.

We are to identify our "weakness" and guard against failure.

Just as every person on Earth has a weakest spot physically, so has every person on this Earth a weakest spot spiritually.

Because, we read of the "Woman", we are made aware of the nature of the Devil's mode of attack:

The Devil attacks on the level of Sex and Materialism, which is mostly reflected in Money.

He also uses Adversity. In other words, he puts Man and Woman under Stress.

The question now arises, how can the Woman know right from wrong, before she has eaten from the Tree of knowledge of Good and Evil?

How can she be held accountable for her possible ignorance?

The answer lies in the Fact, that GOD has bestowed upon Man the ability to choose right from the Beginning. GOD has given Man a Conscience to work with.

Only persistent denial of Right and Wrong will kill Man's Conscience.

When the Conscience has died, the good works of Man have died and Man becomes an instrument of Death.

The evidence is all around us.

Man becomes more and more educated and premature Death is on the increase.

Unconscionable Man commits unconscionable atrocities against his fellow Man.

Gen.
Ch.03;04-05:
04: But the Serpent said to the Woman, "You will not die.
05: for GOD knows, when you eat of it your Eyes will be opened, and you will

be like GOD, knowing good and evil".

The issue here is Death.

The Bible identifies Satan as the originator of Death, (Heb.02;14) but in spite of the Evidence all around us, the Devil denies this Truth.

The first step in the devils strategy against Man is to pretend that he is on Man's side.

He offers Man a bright future and ensnares Man into a state of denial between right and wrong.

As we said before, the devil is very clever, he knows that constant denial of right and wrong dulls Mans conscience or even kills it.

GOD says, when your conscience dies, you will also die with it.

You will die in your sins and have to give account.

This has not changed since the beginning, but the devil says the opposite, because he is the opponent to GOD.

The devil makes false promises. He says, your Eyes will be opened.

He promises, that you will know good from evil, when he actually leads Man to deny it.

The Serpent likes nothing better, than to mislead Man into believing that he can play God and decide on his own what is right or wrong for him.

Jesus says;"If anyone keeps my Word, he will never taste death".(John 8;51)

Man on his own is doomed to fail.

Man, who trusts GOD and Jesus Christ remains on save Ground, physical as well as spiritual.

Gen.

Ch.03;06-07:

06: *So, when the Woman saw that the Tree was good for Food, and that it was a delight to the Eyes, and that the Tree was to be desired to make one wise, she took of the Fruit and ate; and she also gave some to her Husband and he ate.*

07: *Then the Eyes of both were opened, and they knew they were naked; and they sewed Figleaves and made themselves aprons.*

This Spectacle repeats itself with every Human being entering this World, the Garden.

When the Human being is born, enters this World, he or she has no knowledge of good and evil, of right and wrong.
The New-born is innocent.
Although human nature is not described as all good, it is innocent to start out with.
The Bible says, that the New-born is written in the Lambs Book of Life.
Jesus said, the Kingdom of GOD is theirs.
Then, as Man gains knowledge of right and wrong and makes conscious choices in his behavior, his name gets blotted out.
Innocence is no longer his attribute.

This is why GOD has provided a "Redeemer".
This is why GOD has send his Son, Jesus Christ into this World to provide Redemption to all who believe in Him.
Jesus Christ has the Power to reinstate Man back into the Book of Life with a New Name, the New Name replacing the old one, because it has too many bad Memories attached to it.
This was not known at the Beginning, but is now fully revealed (Eph.03;4-5).
Scripture speaks of GOD ordaining Jesus Christ to provide Salvation to all of Mankind before the World was created, meaning His Sacrifice is acceptable to GOD covering all the Ages (Proverbs 08; 22-31).

Here we read, that Man and Woman stooped down to the level of the Serpent.
They did so, because they had a great Desire to know better.
This is an ongoing problem in Humanity ever since.
The Immature want to know more than the Mature.
The Inexperienced want to know better than the Experienced.
Man constantly strives for "Instant Knowledge".
GOD on the other hand keeps Man out of Trouble by revealing to him (her) step by step what Man is ready to learn and is ready to comprehend and what is truly of Benefit to him (her).
Unfortunately, Man wants to be wise ahead of his Time and follow his carnal desires instead of good advise, contained in the immutable, trustworthy Word of GOD.
The unfortunate Results are not far from anyone.

Man is getting smarter and things are getting worse.
According to this Story, it starts on an individual basis and winds up as a collective Enterprise.
This is how the Devil operates.
He starts with the Individual and then drags in the Others.
"Both their Eyes were opened", means, both conspired together and both experienced the same Fate.

When Man relies on his Smarts only and discards the Word of GOD, he winds up with some unexpected Results.
In spite of any acquired Knowledge, Things go unexpectedly wrong.
High Science is no cure-all for all of Mans ills.
Man has Trouble to comprehend, what it means, "the Day you eat from it, you will die".
Many lives can be saved by adhering to good advise, contained in the "Word".
In the Eyes of God, Man has only "Figleaf" solutions (make-shift solutions).
Man expects High Science to cure everything, when in fact he is fiddling around with "Figleaf-aprons". We are speaking of Mans behavior, which can not be substituted with any scientific formula.
Mystery of Mysteries, Man rather does it his way and dies, instead of following life-saving ordinances by GOD.

GOD has pointed out the solution to all of Mans problems, but Man is reluctant to hear it. To eat the forbidden Fruit spells Trouble.
To bear Fruit of Repentance provides Healing.
Man can not have it both ways.
There is a way of Salvation and there is a way which leads to Death.

Choose one and avoid the other.

Gen.
Ch.03;08:
08: And they heard the sound of the Lord GOD walking in the Garden in the cool of the Day, and the Man and his Wife hid themselves from the presence of the Lord GOD among the Trees of the Garden.

Much Wisdom is found in this Verse.

GOD is Spirit and while the Bible speaks of Heaven, the dwelling Place of GOD, it also speaks of GOD walking in the Garden, the Garden where Man is to be found.

In other Words, in all of Mans Misery, he is not alone.

Man can hear the Sound of GODs presence.

The cool of the Day is the opposite to scorching heat.

The Bible teaches Man to stay out of the heat. Does Man get the Message?

Here, we read, that as much as Man and Woman got themself into hot Water,

GOD is merciful in that HE grants them an escape in the cool of the Day.

In the Book of Revelation we read, that Man who has come into the presence of GOD, has come out of great Tribulation.

Then, we read, that Man who has Faith in Jesus Christ is re-instated into the presence of GOD, the cool of the Garden (Rev.07;14-17).

It says, that no longer shall Man be exposed to any scorching heat and that GOD Himself shall protect them.

If Man could only understand, what GOD has prepared for Man, Man could come clean through Faith in GOD and His Son, Jesus Christ and no longer have to go into hiding.

This Story tells of a great misconception by Man:

When Man gets himself into trouble, he wants to find his own solutions, ignore GOD and worse yet, literally hides himself from the presence of GOD.

The Bible clearly teaches, that there is no Hiding-place before GOD, not even behind the Trees of the Garden.

No Infrared lens can match the Eyes of GOD. GOD can see Man, no matter where he hides out.

Trying to hide out before GOD is therefore a total exercise in futility.

It would be better for Man to face his Maker in the "Garden", than from a Place from which there is no return (Hebrews 09;27).

Gen.

Ch.03; 09-10:

09: But the Lord GOD called the Man, and said to him,
    "Where are you?"

10: And he said,
    "I heard the Sound of Thee in the Garden, and I was afraid, because I was
    naked; and I hid myself".

Lets make no mistake about it, the Lord GOD knows where you are.
He knew where you are even before you were there, but there is a reason for
Him calling for you.
What is the reason?
HE, the Lord GOD is calling you to call you out of your state of Denial.
GOD wants you to acknowledge where you are.
This, of course, is not easy for you, because you don't want to confront the
Situation.
You want to do Business as usual.
You are afraid, because you don't want to change, because, deep down you
know your shortcomings (nakedness).
You know, what is the right thing to do, but you are hiding out.
Granted, hiding out can protect you, but hiding out from GOD can not.

Surrender your Life to Him, who can truly protect you.
Surrender your Ego, Yourself.

Gen.

Ch.03;11

11: He said,
    "Who told you that you were naked?
    Have you eaten from the Tree of which I commanded you not to eat?"

Man acknowledges his shameful (naked) condition.
A child can not acknowledge to be naked due to its Innocence.

Why is GOD so concerned with Mans state of Innocence?
Because Innocence is a protective condition.
The child is unaware of nakedness because the child does not know any better.

The Tree of Knowledge is always there.

The child can not avoid it!

Sooner or later, the child is confronted with learning about right and wrong.

This is where the Commandments by GOD come into play.

Because GOD can not approve of Man committing things for which he can not account, GOD commanded Man to obey His Commandments long before Man did anything wrong (Gen.02;16).

But Man dislikes to obey GOD, not realizing, that when he disobeys GOD, he obeys the great Deceiver, the Serpent.

This is the great Controversy in the Human Race.

As soon as the Human being loses his (or her) Innocence, he (or she) starts to obey One or the Other.

In the Book of Revelation, we read of scolding words on this Issue.

We read, that because of Mans disobedience to Christ, he becomes spiritually poor, blind and naked (Rev. 03;17).

Of course, much more can be said about it.

So, we concern ourselves with the Solution to this unavoidable Dilemma, more or less, one might say.

The solution to this age old Dilemma is Jesus Christ according to Holy Scripture.

Christ has come into this World to solve this problem, because Man is unable to solve it by himself.

Jesus Christ offers Man an Escape.

He says: "I council you to buy from me Gold refined by Fire, that you may be rich, and white Garments to clothe you and to keep the shame of your nakedness from being seen and Salve to anoint your Eyes, that you may see (Rev.03;18).

This is very interesting, because in this Story, we read that the Eyes of them both were opened and they knew that they were naked.

We read this in a negative way.

In Revelation, we read that we are wise to permit Christ to anoint our Eyes, so we can see and keep our own nakedness from being seen, namely by GOD.

What does this mean?
It means that Man without GOD is spiritually blind.
When the blind are leading the blind, they both fall.
This is the Story. This is of what we read here. They both fell.
Christ opened and still opens the Eyes of the blind, physically, but more so spiritually.

The Bottom line is this:
When Man walks on his own, he may know right from wrong, but he will fall.
When Man walks with Christ and believes in Him, his Eyes are opened and in spite of his human nature and his human shortcomings, he has acquired Eternal Life as it exists in "Eden".
Jesus Christ has promised: "Today, you shall be with me in Paradise" (Eden).

This should be very comforting.
There is a Paradise of GOD. You can find it Today.

Gen.
Ch.03; Vs 12: *The Man said, "The Woman whom thou gavest to be with me, she gave me Fruit of the Tree, and I ate".*

The first step after the Fall is Blame-shifting.
Man, who is supposed to have acquired "Knowledge" by now, is actually demonstrating Ignorance.
He abrogates his responsibility to the Woman.
He can not reason it out, that with his Blame shifting, he is actually degrading himself.
Not only is the Man ignorant enough to blame his Spouse, he actually blames GOD Himself.
"If You wouldn't have given me the Woman, this could not have happened", he says.
So, the Saga continues, Man is getting smarter, but not any wiser.

GOD is NOT the Cause of Mans Troubles, Man is.

The Woman is neither better nor worse.
The Woman is part of a Joint-venture which has not ended yet.

Gen.
Ch.03;13: Then the Lord GOD said to the Woman, "What is this that You have done?" The Woman said, "The Serpent beguiled me, and I ate".

Each Person shall get his or her turn before GOD,
You can count on it.
GOD absolutely, does not leave anyone out.
Whether we believe it or not, the Bible says, "All must give Account".

Man is not short of Excuses when things go wrong.
Man does not like to be accountable.
Man likes to pass the Puck.
Man is very quick to take credit for his accomplishments, but very slow to step up to the Plate, when he makes a Mess out of things.
Man likes to argue his own point of view, but before a Holy GOD only Truth prevails.
GOD may reason with Man, but GOD does not argue with Man.
GOD is GOD and has the right to ask the Question, however uncomfortable to Man or Woman and there is good reason for GOD to question Man, because the entire Bible speaks of the Deeds of Man following him to the other Side.

Mans (Womans) Deeds do not magically disappear, make no Mistake about it.

Gen.
Ch.03; 14-15:
14: The Lord GOD said to the Serpent,
"Because you have done this, cursed are you above all cattle, and above all wild animals; upon your belly you shall go, and dust you shall eat all the days of your life.

15: I will put enmity between you and the Woman, and between your seed
   and her seed; he shall bruise your head, and you shall bruise his heel".

Unlike Man, GOD reveals His Intentions, the Serpent does not.
To listen to the Serpent is foolhardy at best. We shall see, why.

Here, we read about the nature of the great Serpent, the Devil.
The nature of the Devil is a beastly nature, an animalistic nature, if you
will.
When Man and Woman listened to the Devil, they committed a "Wrong"
in the Eyes of GOD.
Every time, Man commits a "Wrong", he writes the Devil a Cheque and the
Devil will surely cash it. He wont loose it, you can count on it.
This is a Curse in the Human Race.
When Man listens to the great Deceiver, he obeys his carnal nature.
This means, Mans carnal nature is a beastly nature, here identified as
"Wild" and above all Animals.
The Apostle Paul said: "Their belly is their god".
When Mans carnal urges are more important, than the Word of GOD,
Man has become a Servant in the Devils Empire.
A Servant, Man is.
He either serves GOD, lives in the Image of GOD or he serves the Devil
with his beastly nature.
This means, Man has higher Instincts and Man has lower Instincts.
He can not shake either one of them off.
He can only choose, which one dominates his Life.
Even the most godly person has to deal with his lower Instincts. He can not
get out of it, not in this World in all the Days of his Life.
Man is Earth-bound by his carnal nature and can only be Eden-bound by
the Love of GOD in Christ, Jesus.
Jesus Christ spoke of Himself as of the "Son of GOD" and as of the "Son of
Man", here called, the Seed of the Woman.

But there is Enmity between the Seed of the Woman and the Serpent.

The Devil is the originator of Death.
Jesus Christ is the Door to Eternal Life.

Man can not follow both at the same time.
He can only follow One or the Other at any given Moment.

In the book of Revelation we read about two distinctly different Women.
The persecuted Woman who is carried into a spiritual Dessert (this World)
and the glamorous Woman riding on the Beast, meaning, on Mans beastly
nature.

Man belongs to one Woman or the other.
This is the Story here.
It is not a Story ending in Mans Choices, it is a Story laying Mans Choices
before him.
All this does not happen without any "Bruises". It is a daily occurrence.
Even when "saved", Man is engaged in this Enmity between Christ and the
Devil, but only in Jesus Christ can he have Victory.
Only in the Image of GOD can the Higher have Dominion over the Lower.

Gen.
Ch.03;Vs 16: To the Woman He said, "I will greatly multiply your Pain in
child-bearing; in Pain you shall bring forth Children, yet your
desire shall be for your Husband, and he shall rule over you".

This Verse speaks of a Rule.
Beforehand, we saw the Woman and the Man engaged in a Joint-venture.
Here, we see the Rule of Individual accountability.

There is Collective accountability and there is Individual accountability.
The Bible speaks of both.

Revelation says, that how we measure up before GOD has to do with how
we measure our self, but it also says, that when Man is with GOD, there
shall be no more Pain.
Here, we read, that in this Age, this is not possible.
Man is forever looking for ways how to live without Pain and how to die
without Pain.
While Man has come a long way to deal with physical Pain, there is little
success in dealing with emotional Pain.

This Scripture here speaks of both.
It speaks of physical Pain, such as in Child-bearing and it speaks of emotional Pain, such as someone lording it over you.

The Issue is Pain!

No-one on Earth can avoid Pain entirely.
No Woman would elect a Relationship with a Man for the purpose of suffering Pain and yet, it is an inevitable by-product in any and even the godliest of Relationships.
Plainly stated; Life is not without Pain on the entire face of the Earth.
A Relationship may be a happy one, but it will not be able to avoid certain Pain.

This Principle applies also to the Church of Jesus Christ.
We read of those, who have come out of "Great Tribulation", meaning the Church will get "bruised".

So, it was and it is with all the Generations of Man since the Beginning.
Mankind has to deal with Pain, Individually, but also Collectively.

Gen.
Ch.03;17-19:
17: And to Adam He said,
   "Because you have listened to the Voice of your Wife, and have eaten from the Tree of which I commanded you, you shall not eat of it,' cursed be the Ground because of you; in toil you shall eat of it all the days of your Life;
18: Thorns and Thistles it shall bring forth to you; and you shall eat the Plants of the Field.
19: In the sweat of your Face you shall eat Bread, till you return to the Ground, for out of it you were taken; you are Dust and to Dust you shall return".

Now, it is Adams turn.
He does not get away very easy.
He has to deal with a whole litany of repercussions.

Why is that so?

Because, Adam has proven to be a Hypocrite.
Adam has taken a licence from GOD to lord it over his Wife, while at the same time, he listened to her.
In other Words, what he has done, he has done, because she said so.
This scenario repeats itself every day.
The Lord however, is not very fond of Hypocracy.
The Lord wants Man to stand up and be counted. We are talking foremost about spiritual matters and not trivial ones at that.
We are talking about conscious Decisions, Decisions in regards to the Commandments by GOD and pleasing her or for a matter of fact, him.
When we prefer to please a Human being instead of pleasing GOD, we are about to suffer certain Consequences.

This Scripture is as much of an End-time Prophecy as it is a Story of the "Beginning".
Scripture explains very clearly, that toward the end of this Age, Humanitarian Values take precedence over spiritual Values.
GOD is left out of the Equation. Pleasing human Nature comes first.
Human rights have already ascended to unprecedented levels.
The Criminal has more Rights than the Victim.
Try to obtain Information on anything or anyone and you run into barrier after barrier of so-called privacy-rights.
All this in the face of Governments knowing everything about you.
Hypocracy to the highest decree

Another Sign of the close of this Age is the accelerating growth of the Tree of Knowledge.
The Devil waters this Tree a lot, because he knows, that when Man places his Trust in the Tree of Knowledge, instead of the Gospel of Jesus Christ, he is subject to spiritual death.

Here is what is in store for those, who decide to be a Servant in the Devils Empire:
*   A thorny road of Disappointments lies ahead of them.
*   The Days of their Life are measured by what they eat and drink

(deranged Lifestyles).
* Wars are fought over what comes out of the Ground (economic cross-roads).
* Man toil in order to take advantage, one over another (deception).
* Famines perplex Mankind (shortages).
* Men are going nowhere in spite of sweating it out (labor in vain).
* The Wealth of the Rich and Famous will suffer sudden loss and turn into Dust (money will burn up) and finally,
* Mans carnal nature has no Future in the Kingdom of GOD, it has been declared "hostile to GOD".

A Transformation is required.
GOD will not pour new Wine into old Wine-skins.
GOD will provide an un-perishable Body for those who drink the Water of Life and eat the Fruits from the Tree of Life.

We will read more about it.

Gen.
Ch.03;20-21:
20: The Man called his Wife's name Eve, because she was the Mother of all Living.
21: And the Lord God made for Adam and for his Wife garments of Skins, and clothed them.

It is interesting to note, that this Scripture portrays God as a providing GOD, but not as a controlling GOD as far as the human Race is concerned. The Call is on Man.
Why? Because Man is able to identify the nature of his World.
"Eve", stands for human Life.
This implies, that Man is ordained to respect Life, but that Man is also ordained to control Life (call it by name).
In order for Man to name Life and to exercise this GOD given control over it, he has to have a high decree of Understanding about it.
GOD is the Creator of Life, but Motherhood is the essence of Procreation.

Uncontrolled Pro-creation is not found in Scripture.
Nowhere does it say, that uncontrolled reproduction is a blessing.

Man and Woman, who understand this Scripture, please GOD by their ordained ability to reproduce in harmony with their World around them.
Self-control is of course a requirement along this line.
For a matter of Fact, Self-control is a Biblical Virtue.

Now, when Man understands his Calling by GOD, he is ready for new Attire from GOD.
New Attire from GOD is never a makeshift solution like that of Figleaves.
When GOD clothes Man, He goes to the very Skin of it.
He clothes Man and Woman in His Love and His Righteousness.
Will Man accept it ?

Mans Deeds of Righteousness are the proof of the Power of his Love.

Gen.
Ch.03;22-24:
22: Then the Lord GOD said,
   "Behold, the Man has become like us, knowing Good and Evil; and now,
   lest he put forth his hand and take also of the Tree of Life, and eat and
   live forever"-
23: therefore the Lord GOD sent him forth from the Garden of Eden, to till
   the Ground from which he was taken.
24: He drove out the Man; and at the East of the Garden of Eden He placed
   the Cherubim, and a flaming Sword which turned every Way, to guard
   the Way to the Tree of Life.

This Story contains an apparent Contradiction.
It speaks of the Tree of Life in a prohibitive way, when before-hand it spoke of the Tree of Life as an Invitation to treat (you may freely eat from it).

What is the meaning?
Man and his Conscience (knowing good and evil) is the Issue.
The Child has no Conscience, does not know good from evil.
The Child is not sent forth from the Garden of Eden.
The innocent Child has free access from the Garden to Eden, the Kingdom of GOD. It does not have to eat from the Tree of Life to live forever.
Only when knowledge of Good and Evil replaces Innocence, becomes Man

accountable for his actions to GOD.

It does NOT say, that Man can not eat from the Tree of Life.
The Invitation stands.
What it says, is that Man can not obtain eternal Life independently of
GOD.
Eternal Life does NOT exist outside of Eden.
The Garden and Eden are not the same Place.
The Garden of Eden means a connection between the Carnal and the
Spiritual.
The innocent human Being has this unrestricted connection, this
unrestricted access.
The accountable human Being has lost this connection, he or she has
become confined to the Ground, held captive to his (her) carnal Nature.
Carnal Man is separate from a Holy GOD.
Between Eden and the Garden, which now, no longer is of Eden, stands a
Spirit-being and a flaming Sword.
This Story identifies this Spirit-being as a Guardian.
It does NOT say, that Man can not get by this Guardian and the flaming
Sword.
What it says is that Man can not do it by himself.

The flaming Sword is the Word of GOD.
The Tree of Life referres to Eternal Life (live forever).

This Scripture explains, that no-one can get around it – the Word of GOD.
Every accountable Person has to face it, like it or not.
The East of the Garden means, where the Morning Star rises (2.Peter 01;19).
The Bible proclaims, that Jesus Christ is this Morning Star.
We read, that when Man accepts the Word, this Morning Star rises in his
Heart and access to a Great Inheritance (Eden) is assured.
An Inheritance however, it is!

The carnal body has become hostile to GOD because of its sinful nature
and can not inherit Eden without a transformation first.

The Apostle Paul clearly states:

Man who believes in GOD and His Son, Jesus Christ shall be "changed" in the twinkling of an Eye, whether dead or alive (1Cor.15;51-56).

Man must change Now to be transformed by GOD later.
There is no other Way.
All Others shall face Judgement in the second Resurrection (Rev.20;11-15).
Only by the Word of GOD, Jesus Christ, can Man re-enter Eden.
Without the "Word" (flaming Sword), there is no access, make no Mistake about it.
The Tree of Life is available. Eternal Life exists, but GOD does not force His Pardon on anyone. Man can choose. He can choose Life or he can ignore it, but as we have said before, one thing, Man can absolutely not do, get around the Cherubim and the flaming Sword, which is the Word of GOD.

This Story says so !

CREDITS:

Scripture quotations are from

The Revised Standard Version of the Bible
Copyright 1946, 1952 and 1971 by the Division of Christian Education of the
National Council of the Churches of Christ in the U.S.A.

Used by Permission. All Rights reserved.

Further-more the Writer wishes to acknowledge, that this Book could not
have been written in its present form without Studies of the System Bible
Study by the System Bible Company.

Particularly helpful were the Maps of the John Rudin @ Co. Inc. Chicago
Ill.

Index "How Awesome this Place"

THE LAST DAYS

A Biblical Concept

I am the First and the Last, besides ME there is no God. Isa. 44;06
But you Daniel, shut up these Words and seal them until the Time of the END. Dan. 12;04
In those Days I will pour out my Spirit. Joel 02;29
I will put MY Spirit upon HIM and HE shall proclaim Justice to the Gentiles. Matt. 12;18
The Time is fulfilled. Mark 01;04
HE will declare to You the Things that are to come. John 16;13
Having accomplished the Work which Thou gavest Me to do. John 17;04
If it is My Will, that he remain until I come, what is that to You? John 21;22
And in the LAST DAYS, it shall be, GOD declares. Acts 02;17
I am not ashamed of the Gospel... Rom.01;16
In these LAST DAYS, HE has spoken to us by HIS Son. Hebr. 01;02
As it is, HE appeared once and for all at the End of the Age. Hebr. 09;26
Who by GOD'S Power are guarded by Faith for a Salvation, ready to be revealed in the LAST TIME. 1. Peter 01;05
HE was destined before the Foundation of the World, but was made manifest at the END of the TIMES for Your sake. 1. Peter 01;20
Scoffers will come in the LAST DAYS. 2. Peter 03;03
I was in the Spirit on the Lords Day. Rev. 01;10

COMMENTS

Yes, in this present Age of the Gospel of Jesus Christ, we live in the LAST DAYS.

The LAST DAYS begun with Christ on this EARTH and shall NOT end until the last Soul in the Body of Christ has come in.

Isa.44;06 / Daniel 12;04 / Joel 02;29 / Acts 02;17 / Romans 01;16 / Hebrews 01;02/09;26 / 1. Peter 01;20 / 2. Peter 03;03 / Revelation 01;10.

The Body of Christ (the seven Churches or the seven Spirits of GOD) consists of a very specific Number of Souls, namely a specific number of Hebrew

Believers (symbolically called "First fruits" and "Hundred-fourty-four-thousand",

Revelation 07;04 / 14;10 and 21;17 and a Great Multitude from All Nations. Revelation 07;09.

There is much to be said in regards to this Process, as the Complexity of the Kingdom of GOD is beyond Mans Understanding.

Mans Understanding is limited to the Word of GOD, but is also inexhaustable. Rev 19;13

Scripture assures Man and Woman, that whosoever calls on the Name of the LORD shall be saved. Acts 02;21.

This is a Certainty, irregardless of Mans understanding of the Word of GOD.

The LAST DAYS are not to be confused with Judgement Day.

Further to the above, the LAST DAYS are also mentioned as the Time of building of the Temple of GOD or Spiritual House (1.Peter 02;05), the Time of the Church, the Time of the Seven Churches or the seven Spirits of

GOD, the Time of the Gospel, the Time of Grace (the Witness of the Blood of Christ in Heaven), the Time of the two (other) Witnesses, the Spirit of GOD and the Water of Life on Earth.

Unfortunately, the Last Days also run parallel with the so called End Times, whereby demonic forces are relentlessly on the increase.

Scripture repeatedly states: Let the Righteous be Righteous and the Evil be Evil, meaning, Mankind has a Choice, a Choice which Side to be on.

Scripture identifies Evil as a Mystery, a powerful spiritual force.

Satan is identified as the Prince of the Power of the Air. (Eph.02;02)

Christ himself had to contend with him and so does every Creature on this Planet.

Mankind has only one Hope, namely the saving Power of the Grace of GOD.

When GOD created Man, He bestowed upon Man certain Powers, described as having Dominion.

Man is quick to take credit for his creative Powers, bestowed upon Man by GOD, but Man is also quick to abrogate his Dominion back to GOD when Things go wrong.

The Bible explains, that GOD does not want back what HE has given.

Man has to give Account, no matter what and who can give Account to a Holy GOD without Atonement by Jesus Christ.

This is the ISSUE, particularly in these LAST DAYS.

GOD Almighty offers Life eternal to everyone accepting GOD'S Pardon in Christ, but GOD does NOT force HIS Pardon on anyone, make no Mistake about it.

Satan is the Originator of Death.

GOD is the Originator of Life and Life eternal does NOT exist outside the Pardon of GOD.

Taking human Life is a very complicated Issue, as it is permitted in certain circumstances, such as Self-defense, administration of Justice, circumstances beyond Mans control, but certainly not by motive of Revenge or by motive of interference with the Generations of Man.(We are not talking about controlled vs. un-controlled reproduction here).

However, going too far into these Issues would be digressing from the Concept of the LAST DAYS.

The Writer

Signs of the Last Days
of this present Age

Materialism (Love of Money. Betrayal for monetary reason.)

Occultism and Ancestor-worship.

Paranormal occurrence's (UFO's etc.)

Economic and political crossroad's. (Unstable global economy. Unstable Governments).

Three economic alliances; Europe, Asia and America's. (3 foul Spirit's).

Wars and hostilities (Tribal conflicts).

High Science (accelerated knowledge and technology).

Unconscionable behavior (no repentance). Perverted Justice.

Delusions (lost sense of Reality, Deceptions).

Natural catastrophes (Flood, Storm, Earthquake, Fire).

False Religion's (Prosperity Gospel. Church without Deity. Denial of the
            Cross. Denial of spiritual life after physical death. Believe

in physical reincarnation. New Age philosophy. Cosmic worship. Music which appeals to the lower Instincts.)

Loss of sexual identity (same sex relationship's and blatant immorality).

Godlessness, but also

Proclamation of the true Gospel to all Nations.

Gathering of the Hebrews in the State of Israel, (presently minority only).

Charismatic Leaders, high on Propaganda, (presently shifting Electorate).

Humanitarianism breeding Lawlessness, meaning, loveless Society. (Man of perdition, faked privacy rights).

SURE SIGNS, YET TO COME:

New worldwide Calendar (presently different Calendars).

Recurring Antisemitism (majority of Hebrews to gather in Israel).

Recurring dictatorial Governments. (failing Democracy due to Lawlessness).

Surge of economic prosperity before sudden collapse.

New incurable decease's and plaques in spite of medical advances.

Imitation of Life. (Man claiming to create Life, but imitation only.)

Appearance of the "Beast", meaning beastly nature of Man coming to the fore. The "Beast" and the "Antichrist" are synonymous.

Mark of the "Beast", meaning Computer controlled Societies. (Picture or Image that speaks. No one can buy or sell without it.)

Distortion of Time. People are desperately short of Time. Time is on the Fly.

Ten Nation Alliance of North-South-American Nations with strong ties to the European Block. (Nations out of the Roman Empire, Beast of Sea and Land.)

Many wondrous Discoveries.

Out of control Pollution of Water and Air. Horrible Heat.

Monetary worldwide collapse and horrible War, commencing at the dried out Euphrates River.

Explanation:

The foregoing Signs must appear to bring this Age to a close.
While the return of Jesus Christ can Not be calculated due to concealment from the forces of Darkness, it is nevertheless not going to happen without fulfilment of GOD's Plan.
GOD reveals HIS Intentions to Man by inspired Prophecy, revealed in Scripture.
Also, GOD has ordained HIS Ecclesia to consist of a certain Number of Hebrew Believers and a certain Number of Gentile Believers.
Scripture explains, that the Saints will be engaged on Judgement-day.
Hebrew Saints will judge Hebrews, while Gentile Saints will judge Gentiles.
Scripture speaks of Saints of both groups being of equal standing, but it also speaks of a certain Order of Things.
GOD is a GOD of Order and the return of Jesus Christ is foretold within this Order.
Do not be deceived, Christ does not return until the Man of perdition has had his way, although Christ may call You to appear before HIM at any Moment in Time.
The Church better be prepared for troubled Times, because conditions on

Earth will be the worst, they have ever been since the beginning of Time. This is clear prophecy by Jesus Christ himself. (Matthew, Chapter 24).

Those, who claim a smooth sailing toward the End of this Age, lead Man astray.

The two Witnesses are the Spirit and the Water (of Life).

They will take a last surprising global stand, after their apparent absence in the Last Days. There will be a last powerful "knock" on the door by Christ before the Church will go up hither and Christs subsequent return.

Each Letter to the seven Churches speaks of "those, who conquer".

This, unfortunately implies unfavorable conditions for the Church toward the End of this Age.

While a great Reward is in store for all, who endure, certain suffering by the Saints can not be avoided.

The Writer